Helping Laity
Help Others

The Pastor's Handbooks

Helping Laity Help Others

Stanley J. Menking

The Westminster Press
Philadelphia

Scripture quotations from the Revised Standard Version of the Bible
are copyrighted 1946, 1952, © 1971, 1973 by the Division of Christian
Education of the National Council of the Churches of Christ in the
U.S.A., and are used by permission.

First edition

Published by The Westminster Press®
Philadelphia, Pennsylvania

PRINTED IN THE UNITED STATES OF AMERICA

9 8 7 6 5 4 3 2 1

Library of Congress Cataloging in Publication Data

Menking, Stanley J., 1932–
  Helping laity help others.

  (The Pastor's handbooks)
  Includes index.
  1. Lay ministry. I. Title. II. Series.
BV4400.M43 1984   253   83-26061
  ISBN 0-664-24615-X (pbk.)

To the laity of the
United Methodist Churches
in
Mitchell and Pelican, Louisiana
Carley Brook, Girdland, Smith Hill, and Torrey,
Pennsylvania
Old Forge, Pennsylvania
Cranbury, New Jersey
and
Haddonfield, New Jersey
whose commitment to Christ and helping others
taught me the meaning of the ministry of the laity

Contents

Preface   9

Introduction   11

1. Spiritual Preparation of the Pastor   17

2. Creating a Climate for Lay Ministry   27

3. Equipping the Pastor to Equip Laity   39

4. What Is Possible Where You Are?   51

5. Designing a Lay Ministry   63

6. Recruiting and Training Laity   75

7. Organizing to Support Lay Ministry   87

8. Paying for the Ministry   99

A Word of Encouragement   111

Index   113

Preface

It is impossible to thank everyone who has contributed to this book. Some should be noted without being held responsible for my conclusions.

This book is possible because of the invitation of Charles A. Sayre to help the laity of the Haddonfield United Methodist Church help others. I welcome this opportunity to express my appreciation to the many people who lived and worked in an area of Camden, New Jersey, known as North Camden, for all they taught me during the eleven years of my ministry there.

The work of many clergy from across the country in Drew's doctor of ministry program has been valuable in testing my insights on the basis of their experience in helping laity help others.

I want to thank Carolyn Fagan, Barbara Melcher, and Dawn McDermott for their assistance in preparing the manuscript. I appreciate the helpful suggestions of Thomas C. Oden, Charles A. Sayre, Kay Ferrell, Leonard Rowell, and Marion Poindexter, who read the manuscript.

Finally, I want to thank my wife, Betty, and my children, Bonner, Stewart, and Stephanie, who have been supportive of my ministry of helping laity help others long before they had been gracious about the time and help this book required from them.

S.J.M.

The Drew Forest

Introduction

The needs of people in the congregation are always with you as a pastor—couples trying to make marriages work, parents with teenagers on drugs, men and women coping with alcoholism, older people with terminal illnesses, and elderly couples having to move.

Looking at the community where you serve adds to the human needs you see. These may include conflicts over political issues, environmental problems in the community, discriminatory practices, or a local mental health program struggling to survive to help many forgotten persons.

Listening to the radio, catching the evening news, or reading the morning paper only reminds you of important world needs. Technological innovations that eliminate and create jobs, tensions between nations, and countless refugees struggling to survive are a few. In your life as a pastor there are more needs than you can address.

You experience a dilemma. There is the awareness of a biblical and theological consensus to help laity serve those who have these needs. Every day people turn to you expecting help from the church. You feel overwhelmed. You are aware of the commitment, knowledge, and skills of the laity. How can you bring the needs of people and the resources of the laity together? How to do this is what challenges you.

This book seeks to provide some answers. However, these answers will be limited to the concern of *how to develop a corporate ministry of the congregation.* By this I mean a ministry to others that becomes one of the programs of the congregation. It is impossible to consider even a few ministries in any detail. Therefore I will concentrate on generic issues that most lay ministries will face. The book's objective is to help busy pastors by providing them with guidelines and questions that will be useful in most settings. The ministries and results will vary. Some will develop child care centers for working parents. Others will establish a program to aid teenage runaways. Some will work on a state gambling referendum, and some will work with a network of people across the world on environmental issues. You may work on a different need. *The premise of this book is that guidelines exist that can aid most service ministries.*

There are no few easy steps that can be given. Instead, there are ways to use limited time and resources effectively.

This book has a modest purpose. It will suggest specific ways to integrate this task with your other pastoral duties. You will have to commit time to this responsibility, but it will be time well spent.

Helping laity to help others is a significant ministry. You will never be able to do all you would like to do. Your hopes will exceed your achievements. Nevertheless, your ministry, linked with others, can be seen as one way the will of God is at work in the world.

Eight concerns will be examined in this book. In your experience of ministry they will not be neatly separated. We look at each separately for ease of examination and future reference.

> Spiritual preparation
> Establishing a positive congregational climate
> Preparing to help laity help others
> Discovering the needs that can be met
> Developing a realistic and challenging ministry
> Recruiting and training laity
> Creating the appropriate organization
> Paying for the ministry

In 1966 I was given the opportunity to act on my theological conviction to help laity help others. I heard many saying I ought to do it. Others told me what to do. None told me how. What follows is the result of reflecting on that eleven-year experience to discover what would be true for any ministry. These results have also been tested with pastors working on doctor of ministry projects in many settings and on diverse needs. They work!

I assume you believe that helping laity help others is important to your ministry. I want to assure you that it is possible for you to achieve this, and I believe the suggestions that follow will contribute to the realization of this in your ministry.

Helping Laity
Help Others

I

Spiritual Preparation
of the Pastor

A congregation's ministry to serve others can only reach its potential with committed pastoral leadership.

Therefore, to ask you about the maturity of your spiritual life is not an invasion of your privacy. Instead, it acknowledges that your spiritual health is a significant resource for effective lay ministry.

This is a profound theological concern which poses some soul-searching questions.

Will I have the theological hope to go on when a lay service ministry to others does not do all that I planned?

Can I be sustained by a conviction that faithful service counts for more than the numbers of people served?

Is it possible for me to value the ministry of service when it is dismissed by the experts of the world?

Am I willing to commit the time required to help lay-people help others with all I am called upon to do?

Do I trust God's promise that if I am faithful to a vision of laity serving others it will bear fruit?

Is it possible for me to be content with helping laity who will receive the satisfaction and recognition of having done the serving?

This task of ministry probes to see if your faith is vital, mature, and growing. Wrestling with these questions will be unavoidable but at the same time will be very beneficial.

What Will Keep Me Going?

When you are excited about a new ministry, when people respond to the possibilities of serving others, and when you see results of a ministry in the lives of individuals, you are able to keep going. These experiences are a "spiritual high" which give you needed energy. The test of your spiritual maturity will come when you do not have these experiences. What inner spiritual resources will you be able to draw upon to sustain you then?

There are the traditional answers. The ministry of Jesus Christ provides encouragement. The memory and the reality of our call to serve Christ can be a source of developing a quiet resolution to go on. The disciplines of Bible study, meditation, and prayer do nourish. The need of others may continue to elicit your compassion and commitment. All of these have one thing in common. They help you to view your ministry from a wider perspective than from just your personal feelings and experience. They remind you that a failure to nourish your spirit because you are too busy helping others will be self-defeating. You will risk losing touch with the resources you require when you run and grow weary.

There are other resources that can help you to go on when things do not go well, such as habit, doing your job, or fulfilling your obligations. A sense of duty or a refusal to admit defeat may generate a tenacity to help you continue. These reasons may not be the most satisfying. If they help, they should not be ignored. Commitment to help laity serve others is evaluated by fidelity to our labors and not by the barometer of our feelings.

Your understanding of faith will help you to realize that even experiences of despair, discouragement, and defeat can be avenues of spiritual growth. These experiences which demonstrate your weaknesses and limitations can make you aware of your dependence on God's help and can make you receptive to it. It will remind you that the effectiveness of your ministry is in God's hands.

You will have to forge your answer to the question, "What will keep me going?" No one answer will serve all of the time. However, answers can be found that will sustain you. Experience dictates that it must be more than your feelings, the response of the laity, and the ministry's effectiveness in serving others. These are too unreliable and unpredictable. You will have to remain in touch with the reliable and predictable availability of God's promise to sustain those who are called to serve others.

In speaking of a white congregation's ministry in a nearby inner city, a black woman observed, "I have seen people and programs come and go, but after eleven years these people are still here serving." This insight is instructive. What she noted was that "these people" had some inner resource that had enabled them to stay and continue to work at a difficult assignment and help people. What these laypeople and their pastor had that enabled them to keep at it was a commitment to Christ. Their capacity to keep going was a significant witness.

To be able to keep going while helping laypeople help others will require more than activities, though they be many, or successes, though they be great. In the words of Isaiah, "They who wait for the LORD shall renew their strength" (Isa. 40:31). In the end it is this waiting which will enable you to receive the inner resources that will be needed to begin and to continue the task of helping laypeople help others.

Defining the Effectiveness of a Ministry

You, no doubt, believe you should be faithful first and successful second. At the same time, you need to know how the ministry is doing. There is a concern on your part that to ask this question is to capitulate to cultural norms. To ask if lay service to others is effective does not have to be incompatible with your faith.

Numbers are important indicators of an effective ministry. One only needs to note the frequency of questions such as, "How many?" "How much?" or "How often?" We served one hundred meals to shut-ins. This year we raised twice as much money to send inner-city children to camp. Our telephone hotline helped 63 percent of those who called to get emergency aid. You, along with others, pay attention to numbers. They provide answers to help ascertain whether a ministry is reaching and helping people. Responsible stewardship of limited resources will require you to ask if resources are being used wisely.

Many resources may be committed to help one person leave prison and make a new life or for one refugee family to resettle. Here the numbers will seem small. In these two cases the results can justify the investment. Numbers provide one way to help measure effectiveness. They are never the sole criterion.

Everyone wants a quality ministry. The problem is how will the quality of a ministry be determined. Answers will be subjective. The core of this subjectivity—yours, the laity's, those served, or an observer's—is often unarticulated expectations.

A pastor, for instance, decides that because of the large number of corporate executives in the congregation a series of meetings with them to focus on their ministry in the life of the corporation is a way to help them help others. The pastor also hopes they will see the church's ethical concerns as valid and not naive. The laypeople want their pastor to become more knowledgeable about the constraints they face. To obtain an adequate appraisal of whether this ministry fulfills everyone's expectations is not easy. If one of the pastor's goals is to gain an appreciation of what the laity face in trying to help others and this takes place, the pastor will give a high rating to the effectiveness of this effort in terms of quality.

When you seek to answer the question of quality, it is less precise. In the above example the question of quality could also be appraised by the fact that lay attendance at the discussions of corporate responsibility did not fall off. Continued lay attendance would indicate the laity thought they were benefiting from it. By defining ways to answer the questions of quality you avoid the spiritual malaise of thinking you could always be doing better than you are. These questions will be important because they are indicators of effective caring. You need to know how you are helping and how helpful you are to others. You need to know this for yourself as a pastor. You also need to know because the laity will want and need answers, too. Your motivation is not to receive praise but to check effectiveness. *We count because we care. We measure because we want to help.*

No matter how well you do, you must accept the fact that your ministry is never adequate. You will experience a sense of having fallen short. Here you are engaged in a spiritual struggle. You may lower your sights so you will not feel you are failing. This would be to base your ministry on works. Another option is to acknowledge that you still need God's grace even when you are effective. You must live from God's grace on your best days as well as your worst ones. It is to know that you will seldom be able to say, "Today I did it." But you *can* say: "I did my best, Lord. I know it is not all that you want or I want. Yet I trust your promise that you accept this ministry and you will use it. Lord, I will be back tomorrow." What began as a question of the ministry's effectiveness stimulates dealing with the introspective spiritual concern of the pitfalls of pride and despair. This can lead to a new discovery of the reality and practicality of grace in your own life.

Am I Able to Share My Ministry?

The biblical theological consensus about the ministry of laity serving others has not completely permeated the consciousness of the laity. Many laypeople feel they lack a call, training, and authority. They help others, but this is not viewed as ministry. Some laity believe the pastor is paid to do this. Where ministry is still perceived as what a pastor does, it is a challenge to share the ministry dimension of helping others.

There is a realism in lay perceptions. Laity realize they need help with biblical and theological understandings, and training in particular skills. Aware of the limitations of their time laity know that there are constraints on what they can accomplish. In addition, laypersons are all too aware that those they help are appreciative, but they do not always see what they do as being ministry. A pastor does that. You cannot ignore these concerns, but have to work on some and around others.

It is ironic that at a time when there is a greater acceptance by clergy of lay ministry we confront a knowledge explosion requiring more specialists, which works against lay efforts in many areas of life. Any ministry you seek to develop will confront a body of knowledge and a group of experts which call into question how much help a group of amateurs can provide. These concerns cannot be dismissed, but they need not intimidate you.

Your church, for example, may want to create a program to help juvenile first offenders. There are many professionals working with these youth: judges, lawyers, parole officers, social workers, and counselors. It is not just a question of religious novices invading the turf of professionals. Those who work with these young people want to see them helped. They may not question your motives, but they may not trust your abilities. You do have an obligation to learn from the professionals because you agree completely with the goal of helping youth. At the same time, you can affirm the gifts the laity can contribute.

There are inner blocks which will hinder you from sharing your ministry. Your ministry to the dying could be an example. You may believe, for legitimate reasons, that laity cannot do some tasks. Laypeople may lack time, ability, or credibility. You may judge that the needs of some people cannot wait until the laity are able to help. You could use these reasons to avoid training laity. It is important for you to ponder the question, "Is the issue the laity's ability, or is it my inability to surrender this ministry to someone else?"

A lay ministry to others may seem desirable when the task

required is one you do not enjoy. It may be more difficult to start
a lay ministry in an area you enjoy and do well. You may excel
in working with those going through grief. Training the laity for
such a ministry may hinge on the strength of your desire to work
with those in grief. This is a very human trait. You have to
inquire whether there is a correlation between your likes and
dislikes and the lay ministries you want to begin.

There may be a reluctance on your part to ask laypeople to
serve because you fear they may say no. One way of coping with
this fear is never to ask. "Can I really train laity to serve others?" is another concern. Doubt about your ability to train them
may block the development of a needed ministry. A very personal issue is whether you are willing to trust the laity. This may
vary from your insecurities to the realization that laity will be
working with people who are hurting and in need of competent
help. These questions can only be confronted in self-examination. This inner exploration can help you see if the problem is
with the laity, with those being served, or with yourself. The
good news is that if you discover you are the problem, you can
do something about it!

The Burden of a Vision?

The chance of developing a lay ministry to others is possible
if you have a vision. It does not have to originate with you, but
you must make a commitment to a vision if a lay ministry to
others is to be developed in your congregation.

Having a vision is not a mass experience. It is usually a
lonely one. You see needs many do not seem to notice. You
may have a vision of a ministry to help battered women. Your
vision, however, is evaluated not by new possibilities but by
old perceptions. Your vision is greeted by skepticism even
when people believe the realization of the vision would be
beneficial. To be held responsible for the realization of this
vision seems unfair. It is easier for you to say, "The laity did
not see," than to confess, "I did not enable them to see."

There is no doubt you may resist this. You do not have control over other people's responses. Laypeople are free to reject the vision. In your heart you know this does not relieve you of the responsibility to have, to share, and to work for a vision of ministry. This is the burden and the challenge of your labors as an institutional leader.

Visions take time to realize, and therefore require patience and persistence. For that reason these two questions always have to be asked:

How long will it take to translate this vision into a functioning ministry?

Will I be here long enough to be the midwife for this vision?

Depending on the need, it can take from two to five years to move from a vision of service by laity to a ministry in full operation. Because of this fact, there is often an understandable hesitancy on the part of the laity. It is based on the very realistic assessment of whether or not their pastor will be with the congregation long enough for the vision to develop into a ministry. When the laity ask if you will remain long enough to nurture the vision to life, they are being very pragmatic. Should your answer be no, it would be better not to start. If your answer is yes, then it is appropriate to proceed.

Am I Prepared to Wash Feet?

The image of ministry as servant has a long history and a biblical basis that commends it. This has not always been the dominant option. The herald image sees the pastor as a preacher of the word, with the laity as the hearers. The sacramental image views clergy as celebrants and laity as recipients. In the twentieth century the servant image that sees the pastor as one who helps the laity help others has gained prominence.

This theological shift can bring psychological and spiritual

difficulties to its most faithful adherents. It is no easier for you
to conform to this image than it was for the first disciples. That
it is biblical may not make it easier. It may mean it is more
difficult because it cannot be easily dismissed.

You acknowledge the gospel's claim on your life. So when
you make sacrifices, seek to keep your own needs under control,
work to give yourself for others, and then are not appreciated
or respected, you may have to struggle with anger: anger at
others, at yourself, and at God. After all, it is certainly reasonable for you to expect that your efforts deserve a word of appreciation.

A pastor had labored long and hard to involve laypeople in
seeking open housing in a suburb, with some success. Then in
a meeting he was accused of being racist and not doing enough!
No word of appreciation was spoken. Those who rejected him
did not even ask what had been done. He wanted to walk away
from it all. In the depths of his heart he knew that the spiritual
struggle about being willing "to wash feet" was at hand.

You do have skills, knowledge, and wisdom to help laypeople
help others. They may be perceived by others as idealistic, naive,
or out of touch. That does not mean you are wrong or unrealistic. You may feel resentment when this happens. You may
wonder what has been gained in standing for a point of view and
being ignored. Bitterness can capture your heart. Then you may
ask, "What have I gained if obedience to a vision of laity serving
others leaves me resentful?" Coming to terms with these feelings
is tough! These moments bring home to you the awareness that
your spiritual struggle is with principalities and powers within
as well as with the forces of self-regard in the world.

Many have tried to discover a contemporary image that expresses some elements of the biblical servant image. One that
has been used is that of coach, the one who serves the players
by preparing them to play the game. Some ministers have
wanted to modify the image to that of player-coach. It is never
easy to give up the excitement of being the doer of ministry. The
dominant issue here is not who will get the credit. Good coaches

and good pastors both get credit. What you may miss the most is the action, the ministry. In the end, however, the problem is still spiritual. It is the issue of obedience to your call to help laity help others.

The question of your willingness "to wash feet" is not only a call for you to express your faith. It also stimulates the development of your faith. This is neither easy nor automatic. It will goad you to grow. It will drive you to seek the help of others. It will invite you to seek God's guidance and strength. Your spiritual development can be one of the benefits from seeking to help laity help others.

At times you will feel completely drained, at other times enriched. In the end the task of helping laity help others will give more than it requires. There will be difficulties, but in time you will discover that your efforts will be personally rewarding because the difficulties will be surmounted and they will have stimulated a maturing of your faith that could not have come to you without them.

The creation of a ministry to help laity help others means you must begin by engaging in self-examination. Inner wholeness is a prerequisite to outer effectiveness. Before, during, and after assuming the responsibility to help the laity, you will have to look within and come to terms with yourself over and over again. As long as this struggle is in process spiritual growth will be stimulated. What you first perceived as a task of ministry will, at the deepest level of your life, be experienced as a real spiritual pilgrimage.

2

Creating a Climate
for Lay Ministry

You can create a climate to encourage laity to serve others
with a minimum of extra effort. Your place in the local church
provides a unique opportunity to orchestrate a positive climate
for lay ministry. It is not always necessary to do new things.
Instead, you can use the time you already spend on worship,
preaching, learning opportunities, and the administration of the
church to accomplish the goal.

Worship That Celebrates Lay Ministry to Others

Using worship to create this climate can be the easiest and the
most difficult thing to do. It is easiest because you are in charge.
It is difficult because you know that people do not like too many
changes too fast. You need to move at a pace that will allow the
laity to make the necessary psychological adjustments. Not all
changes will mean doing new things. It may mean doing old
things in new ways.

Hymns can play an important role in the spirit of the congregation. Luther's "A Mighty Fortress Is Our God" is good when
your ministry is encountering difficulties. "A Charge to Keep I
Have" from Wesley's pen can remind laity that they serve because of Christ's call and not people's responses. When things
do not seem to be going as planned, Cowper's "God Moves in
a Mysterious Way" may reinforce a trust in God's providence.
Those who are not sure about the social gospel may hear a call

to serve in Washington Gladden's fine hymn, "O Master, Let Me Walk with Thee" or Frank Mason North's "Where Cross the Crowded Ways of Life."

People like to sing hymns they know. After examining the hymnal to determine which hymns could be used, you should meet with the organist, the music committee, and a few laypeople to review these hymns. There will always be some excellent hymns you would like to use that the congregation does not know. Select a new hymn each month. The story of that hymn's origin can be shared and the hymn can be used as special music the Sunday before the congregation sings it. Arrange to keep records of which hymns are used to avoid frequent duplication. This way the congregation can sing itself into ministry!

The use of the Bible in worship offers another opportunity to enrich the awareness of lay service to others as part of the church's ministry. In a year there will be many texts that speak to the ministry of serving others' needs. The theme of loving our neighbor is central in the biblical record. The exodus saga delivering Israel from slavery to freedom, the giving of the law that protects all, the prophetic critique of injustice, the word of hope in the experience of the exile, the expectation of a messianic deliverer, the ministry of Jesus, Jesus' calls to discipleship, the caring for the poor and weak in the early church, the detailed discussions of the Christian life-style in the epistles, and the call to be faithful when persecuted in Revelation all relate to this motif. The Scripture lessons could be introduced in a way to point the hearer to this service dimension in the text.

Prayers offer a way to support lay ministry. Congregationaι prayers can direct attention to the needs of others and to those who seek to meet these needs. These prayers should be very specific. For example, in addition to praying for all the hungry in the world, you can pray for those who face hunger in your community because they have no work. Your prayer can relate to a halfway house for the mentally ill in the neighborhood. The fears that those who live there might harm community residents or someone in the community might attack those in the halfway house. The feelings of being uncomfortable with those who live there, not being sure what to do, and the uncertainties of what God is calling us to do can be expressed in this prayer. These times of prayer can help all to hear God's call and discover God's will.

. Announcements offer a place to share concerns for others. Have foster parents share with the congregation their ministry to a child who needed help because she could not live at home. With some imagination, announcements can help create the climate for ministry to others.

Special services are appropriate. You could commission laypeople for ministry in a health clinic or celebrate the anniversary of the church's ministry with a "gamblers anonymous" support group. Since many church meetings begin with worship, it would be possible to include times when they remembered the congregation's lay ministries to scouts, shut-ins, or other special ministries. You can ask laity who are involved in these to create worship services with you for congregational use. This would help those engaged in the ministry to see the relationship of their service and worship. It could also remind the congregation that its ministry to others is a response to worship.

You could invite laity to prepare for and participate in the leadership of worship. Being asked to write or offer a prayer, read a Scripture lesson, or make an announcement that will address the needs of others that the congregation's ministries serve can help laity see this service in its faith context.

Worship is the center of a congregation's life, and it is here that individuals will be able to discover God's personal call to help develop and support a lay ministry which helps others.

Sermons That Inspire Ministry to Others

After serving as a pastor with the responsibility of preaching every Sunday, I joined the staff of a church where my primary responsibility was helping laypeople to create and carry out ministries to others. I was no longer preaching every week. I was again a hearer of the word. I discovered something important about relevant preaching. The proclamation of the gospel is the most basic way for sermons to create a climate that inspires service to others. The gospel has the power to remind hearers of their gratitude for God's love in Christ and to invite them to continue Christ's ministry of serving others. This seems obvious, but because of a concern for others, preaching can shift to telling people what they should do instead of reminding them of what God has done.

The experience of the laity will shape the form and approach of the sermon. If the laity in the congregation stand outside the decision-making process in the world, they may have little confidence that they can influence the course of events. This may be the case for churches in inner-city neighborhoods, depressed communities, declining rural areas, or non-English-speaking congregations. In these settings the sermon needs to stress the promise that God cares, and that their labors to help others are not in vain. Congregations in middle-class suburbs or economically affluent areas where the laypeople are those who exercise power and make decisions that shape the life of governments, business, institutions, and the community will need to hear that God calls people with power to be responsible for shaping the world so that the needs of the powerless are not ignored.

Both of these stances have biblical precedents. The issue with which you will struggle is how to take the experience of the hearer seriously. This will not dictate what the gospel is. However, it will help you to develop sermons that relate the gospel to where you are so your laity can understand it.

It will help if you involve laity in sermon preparation and feedback. Many pastors have done this. In sermon preparation, one approach would be for you to invite six to eight laypersons to meet with you to discuss the texts for the sermons two or three months in advance. You could use the lectionary or select passages to be read. The laity could read a short book or a section from a longer book in the Bible and identify texts to be used for sermons.

What is most helpful is to meet with the laity. This provides you with an opportunity to discuss the texts, to hear concerns of people, and to ask what needs these texts invite you to remember, to share, and to consider as ministries for others. If you did this each year, then you could share the results of these conversations with your congregation. There will be receptivity because of the lay participation.

Feedback sessions are helpful. Too often what you preach and what the laity hear are not the same. Therefore, when a sermon focuses on a need of people, a new ministry to others, or on the role of the laity in meeting these needs, a feedback session is a good plan. You may or may not want to be present. It would help if you were present to hear, to respond, and to clarify. There may be times you should be absent. When the issue in the sermon is very controversial, the laity may only feel free to express their positions if you are not there. If you agree not to ask who expresses points of view, it can give freedom for people to speak while preserving your relationship with them. Feedback sessions are ways to promote communication. As long as you can keep from being defensive, this process can work.

Illustrations in sermons also help. Volumes of statistics or predictions of calamities do not inspire. The stories of people with needs or of laity serving these needs do inspire. Laypeople can relate to the story of a stroke victim who is able to live at home again because of many hours of lay help with the necessary therapy. Telling of a church's ministry when a forgotten older person was discovered, his house repaired, financial help arranged, allowing him to live in his home with dignity in his remaining years, makes service to others come alive in a way that statistics never can.

Stories, of course, must be used with care so that the privacy, dignity, and self-respect of people is not disregarded or damaged. If a story is to be used, you will need to obtain the person's permission or change the names and places to protect a person's privacy. Should there be any serious doubt that the use of the material would harm someone, the story must not be used, no matter how appropriate or effective it would be.

Since the sermon is so central in the life of the congregation, it offers a unique way to create a climate for ministry to others. Already one of your major tasks, it offers a viable way to share a vision of lay service to others without imposing inordinate new demands upon your time.

Learning Experiences That Nurture Ministry to Others

The educational program will, of course, be concerned with more than the specific ministry a local church is considering or doing. At the same time, the educational program can use a ministry of service to others in its curriculum. You can make an important contribution to the role that educational opportunities can have in creating a climate of lay ministry to others.

It needs to be noted that the suggestions that follow will focus on adults. This does not mean you should exclude children or youth in educational planning when considering the congregation's service ministries. Because of the limited space of this book, suggestions will be primarily applicable to adults.

Whether you or another staff person manages the educational program, you will need to use imagination and also encourage the laity with whom you work to use theirs.

One approach is to create short-term studies or projects that can help laity discover the needs of others. Assume that you became aware of a housing problem in the community. How could this need be integrated into the educational program of the congregation? Books could be placed in the church library for reference. Classes, forums, and short-term discussion groups could be created with members and experts invited to serve as leaders or resource persons. A field trip could be set up to visit housing in the community that needs attention or to visit programs in other communities that are working to solve a similar housing need. You could go with a few laypeople to visit persons who need improved housing. Laity could report back to groups studying the housing need. There are often conferences on most issues a service ministry would be addressing. You or some of the laity could attend and take part in workshops on the housing needs being examined. The contacts made at the conference with other people working on the same housing needs would be beneficial. A series of public meetings could be planned for the congregation that would bring in several people over four or five weeks to discuss the housing need from their perspectives. In some instances you might use all of these methods or only some of them. This approach may never go farther than being an educational program. However, if it leads to a service ministry in housing, it will have helped prepare the climate for that to happen.

Every congregation has several networks that are informal communication systems. They function with various degrees of accuracy. For this reason you will want to involve representatives from as many of these networks as you can. What you will be doing is to utilize the grapevine effect of these informal networks. Any new service program will be discussed in the many structured and unstructured groups in the church. Involving representatives of these special networks in various learning experiences can ensure that in most of the informal exchanges taking place in a congregation someone will be present who is aware of the needs the ministry is seeking to meet and has accurate information which can be shared.

A great deal of research has been done in recent years on how adults learn. It is helpful to draw on insights from this work. One thing you could do is to talk to those involved in adult continuing education in order to find out how adults learn. A telephone call to a denomination's educational resource person or a nearby theological school will provide information on current literature in the field. The writings of Malcolm Knowles are considered basic in the field of adult learning and are worth investigating. Copies of his writings may be available in the community library, or the library staff may be able to obtain his books on loan.

Insights from this research remind us that adults learn best by firsthand experience, problem solving, and through discovery. You need to remember that your many years of formal education had a pattern of moving from theory to practice, whereas many laity learn by moving from experience to theory. As a rule, laity are more likely to start with an issue or a special problem, such as the house repair needs of widows in the community, and seek to discover what can be done rather than starting from a more general theoretical discussion of housing or widows. It is better for you to change your approach than to force the laity to shift gears.

Do not seek to guide the laity toward your own preconceived solution. It will have the unfortunate consequence of blocking insights from the experience the laity bring to the need being explored. Likewise, it will hinder the emergence of new creative solutions that can happen only if you remain open to options other than your own.

By having patience to wait, you will create a climate that supports a ministry of service to others and generates more effective ways of carrying out the ministry as a result of this input. These educational approaches will help contribute to the laity's ownership of the service ministry.

Administrative Practices to Encourage Ministry for Others

Creating an effective lay service ministry to others is a political process. At its best it seeks to gain endorsement through a consensus-building process. Since this takes time, it will require self-discipline from you and from the laity working with you.

This means you will need to have many one-to-one conversations with laypeople to sow seeds, to take their pulse, to discover their questions and problems in order to begin a significant lay ministry to help others that will be supported. This lays good groundwork.

Pastoral calling can play a key role. You will discover past experiences of which you were unaware and which could have an impact on a new ministry. One pastor met resistance to the idea of the congregation buying property for a service project. In a conversation several months later she learned of an unpleasant experience the church had had twenty years before with a property it had owned. That hidden history was the problem, not the proposed project.

It will help you to hear in private conversations the legitimate concerns of laity. It may be the only way you hear of some concerns. These are not ways people drag their feet or oppose helping others. Their concerns will be crucial for the ministry, too. By discovering them early you can do something about them.

You need to know who must be involved in the decision to start a lay ministry. The formal congregational decision process is usually clear. However, there is often an informal process. Laypeople whose judgment, wisdom, reputation, and power can influence a decision cannot be neglected or overlooked, whether they are involved in the formal structures or not. Their endorsement is needed. It may not be forthcoming if they oppose the ministry because of a conviction that it was not well conceived or they were not consulted. Laypeople are genuinely pleased to be asked what they think and feel. After all, it was their church before you came and will be their church after you leave.

The administrative process of developing a lay ministry to others will have to move to the formal decision-making procedures in the administrative structure of the church at some point. How you help this to happen will be crucial.

It is important to avoid surprises. You and a few laity may become concerned about the need for tutoring and after-school care for grade-school children of working mothers in the community. It is a real need. If a new program for the need is presented one evening to the appropriate administrative body for approval with no advance preparation, those who are asked to decide will only feel they are being manipulated. In that case strong resistance should come as no surprise.

It would be prudent to begin by asking for a study group to be formed to report back in one to three months. Using the above case as an example, you could include in this study group people with a background in education, child care, social work, and, if possible, some working mothers. This initial request poses little threat to an administrative body. No decision is being made that involves a long-term commitment. If the study discloses a need, the next step would be to propose creating a task force to design a pilot project. This assignment may be given to the study group, with some new people added, or it could be given to an entirely new group of people. It can take from one to three months more before a proposal can be submitted. Once the design with the costs is developed, it would be possible to request authorization from the appropriate administrative bodies for a pilot project that would take from one to two years.

A pilot project gives valuable time to refine a ministry from limited experience. If the pilot project is effective, it is very easy to adopt it as a permanent ministry of the church. If the pilot project does not work, it can be redesigned and extended or it can be terminated.

This process may seem to be long and involved. It could take from one to three years. However, this process accomplishes two things: it develops a way to explore the needs of others and it helps find creative ways to meet those needs.

Lay ministry must be carried out by the laity. This has implications for an administrative process that cannot be overlooked. Because the laity must understand the ministry, own the ministry, and do the ministry, you cannot prescribe or dictate exactly what this ministry will be. You can only nurture, encourage, and support the process of creating the ministry. Your activity will be directed toward encouraging laity to embrace a ministry to others. The benefit of this approach is that through lay involvement the ministry will take on its own life and may outlive your tenure.

Your efforts to create a supportive climate for laypeople to serve others will seek to maximize the various ways people can participate—from prayers to direct service. Not all of the needs that you discover can be met. The church will not be able to undertake some of them for various reasons. Others that are begun may have a short life. A few will grow and thrive. Therefore, in the long run the most significant long-term results may not be the ministries themselves. Instead, their collective contribution will be to create a climate in which laypeople are invited as well as challenged to help others through various congregational ministries.

3

Equipping the Pastor
to Equip Laity

It is impossible to be able to focus on every human need, but as you assist the laity in helping others you will discover opportunities for personal growth. This makes the task of ministry stimulating. The laity will expect you to help them define their service theologically. This makes the task of ministry satisfying. You will have an important role in preparing laity for a specific ministry that involves the best in theory and in practice. This makes the task of ministry fulfilling.

While much has been written on the responsibility to equip the laity, little has been written on your preparation to do this. It is to this concern that we now turn.

Creating a Theological Rationale for a Ministry

Laity will want your help as they seek to understand helping others biblically and theologically. You will encounter a variety of theological understandings. It is best to identify these points of view from the beginning. *Lay theological understandings will affect the way the laity respond* to every issue that will emerge in the creation of a ministry to others. The basis of a disagreement on a method may really be an expression of theological differences. If these positions are not known, you may miss the fact that the real source of a conflict is theological.

A very dramatic instance would be in a ministry related to abortion. Beyond the positions for or against abortion will be issues of the meaning of creation, guilt, and forgiveness, and the possibility of people changing and making a new beginning which faith calls grace. Theological concerns are also present in issues not as dramatic as abortion. All require theological reflection prior to programmatic development.

Laity will want help in exploring why they should do this ministry, how their ministry fits into God's plan, and how they can interpret it to others as an act of faith. They may not use your theological language, but they will be struggling with basic theological issues. Their questions will require you to articulate your theology of a service ministry. It will require you to break new theological ground as you relate your theology to a particular human need. A vital theological rationale will be the one you work out for and with the laity.

Your laity will not always accept your theological rationale. Nevertheless, they will still expect you to be their primary theological resource. Your sharing, therefore, will provide one way to contribute to their spiritual enrichment. Their need will give an urgent vitality to your theological reflection because of its importance. The theological climate in your congregation will be shaped by your work. While your efforts will provide theological direction for the ministry, your approach to these concerns should invite interaction.

If you achieve this, it will provoke a dialogue with the laity and develop a theological basis for the ministry. This will take time for you to think, to prepare, to present, and to interact with the laity. *Time spent this way is not the prelude to the ministry. It is the first chapter of the new ministry.*

Learning from Others

There are many places to turn for help to find ministries similar to the one you are considering. Denominational executives, agencies, and boards are easy to contact. They may know of ministries you can examine. Another place would be local, county, state, or national health and welfare agencies. If you were seeking to help the handicapped, for instance, you could contact Goodwill Industries. Government agencies may know of some church programs that are effective. If you are interested in prison ministries, you can talk to correction agencies. Once you know where these programs are you will need to contact their leaders. If a ministry is nearby, it may be possible for you to visit it with some laypeople. If a ministry has an excellent reputation, it would be worth spending the time and money to make a visit even if it is some distance away. If it is not possible to make a personal visit, you can make a telephone call. Sometimes bringing a person from an effective ministry to consult with you and your laity can be significant. Writing letters is not effective. The best you can hope for is that you will be sent some helpful material.

You can ask the people you contact the following questions:

How do you understand your ministry theologically?

If you were beginning again, what would you repeat, do differently, do in addition to what was done, or not do?

What has surprised you?

Where are the pitfalls?

What are the commonsense answers that do not work?

What must we do to be effective?

Asking open-ended questions and listening are the best ways to learn from others.

Theological schools and universities are another resource. Helpful persons, often overlooked, are the librarians. They are willing to help you find relevant resources.

It would be wise to talk to those related to a theological school's doctor of ministry program. Since the early 1970s, hundreds of clergy have carried out professional projects, many of which were on how to assist laity in helping others. University Microfilms International (300 N. Zeel Road, Ann Arbor, Mich-

igan 48106) has many such projects on microfilm. Should a
project seem significant, a printed copy can be purchased. The
projects provide examples, have good bibliographies, offer theological rationales, and describe procedures, training, resources,
and experiences that are valuable. Subsequent information, ob-
tained by following up with a personal contact either with the
pastor who did the project or with the congregation where the
project was done, can also be beneficial.

Professors can also be contacted. They may have limited or
extensive firsthand experience. They, too, may know of others
engaged in these ministries. They can aid you in sharpening
your theological perspectives and offering suggestions about
ways to help prepare laity for their ministry.

You will want to begin to build your library and the church's
library. For every service ministry there are a few books that are
classics. Ministries, for example, working with death and dying
will want to have some of Elisabeth Kübler-Ross's writings.
Likewise, there are book clubs for almost every interest; you can
join the ones that are applicable. Subscribing to magazines will
be one way to stay current. To find resources look at literature
in the offices and waiting rooms where you visit on behalf of the
ministry. Government publications are available from local,
state, and national agencies. The problem will not be locating
published materials but finding the time to read them.

Once you focus your attention on an issue, you will discover
television programs, films, and newspaper articles that will relate to your concerns. Laity knowing the church's interest will
begin to bring you information from their reading. You will be
amazed at the information that begins to flow in your direction.

Do not overlook the laity who work or serve in programs
meeting the needs of people. Conversations with these tutors
will be extremely enlightening. They can offer guidance, open
doors, and point out the unique elements that will affect ministry where you are. Their wisdom will help to ensure that the
ministry will avoid the mistakes of inexperience and ignorance.

The Pastor's Learning Agenda

Those who have pressing needs, seek help now! Those who want to help, want to help now! Wanting to help and being helpful are not the same. You have to pursue a learning agenda before you can be effective in helping the laity help others.

A useful discipline you can accept is to make a commitment to develop position papers, lectures, or sermons on the need the laity will meet. Preparing these presentations will help you work through various decisions about the ministry; it will also clarify options and develop ways to explore issues, needs, and opportunities related to this ministry of the laity. If you will set a date to make these presentations and announce it publicly, it will place them on your list of things to do.

There will be many good reasons you can contrive to convince yourself that you do not need to put your thoughts into writing. You will read a great deal, talk to many people, discuss many options. These efforts are important, but they are preparatory. They will help you become familiar with issues, terminology, and resources. You will begin to feel comfortable and sense you are becoming knowledgeable. This is still provisional. You have yet to articulate *your position* publicly in a careful way. When you write and share a position with the laity you accomplish two things. You develop a position, and then discover if you have expressed it so that others can understand it. They may or may not agree with it. That is not the issue. The issue is having a position and being able to articulate it. Experience teaches that in the process of carefully working out your position and getting feedback from others about where you seem unclear, you are making the basic decisions that will provide direction for a ministry which will help others.

An important step is to provide training for the laity. Whether you will do all, some, or little of the training is an open question. You will have to see that a training program is designed around what the laity needs to know.

Most training will take place in small groups. A review of small-group leadership skills or a workshop designed for leaders of small groups will enhance and refresh your knowledge and hone your abilities to work in small-group settings.

Teachers and trainers in your congregation who work with adults will be excellent resource persons. Other pastors or denominational staff persons with skills in training adults should be consulted. They can give ideas for experiential learning, review your training plans, or aid in building a training program for your ministry. People who are involved in organizations, either business or nonprofit, must continuously work on problem-solving techniques. Their experience, background, and knowledge are another resource to be tapped. Because competent practice is as important as a sound theological rationale, you will also want to examine other training programs inside and outside the church to ensure that what you develop will work.

Laity will want clear, specific, and well-defined duties, tasks, responsibilities, and assignments. How to do this will be discussed in a subsequent chapter. The suggestion being made here is that you can gain help in doing this by turning to those who manage others. In addition to literature which can be read, every church will no doubt have laity who manage people. Some may even manage volunteers. All have the responsibility of accomplishing planned results through others. They have experience and wisdom in doing this. Since you will be helping laity to help others, you will be managing, supervising, and delegating. Exploring these issues with laity who have to do this in their work will be extremely valuable to you.

Creating Congregational Ownership

Since you yourself are not seeking permission from your church to serve a special need of others, the question with which you will struggle from the beginning of a lay service ministry is, *What must I do to enable the laity and the congregation to claim this ministry as their own?*

What are the required informal procedures and processes in your church? Who are the people who must either bless or accept the ministry? Every church has long-time members who can give you good advice if you ask them, "If you were going to do this, how would you do it and to whom would you talk?" These unwritten-approval processes and persons hold the key to your beginning a ministry to help laity help others. Who and what they are will be different in each church. It is known that informal approval must precede or accompany formal endorsement if the congregation is going to own the ministry. This means that ownership is not necessarily assured if you have only the formal approval by the decision-making bodies of the church!

As you go about your daily tasks there will be times you can have conversations with laypeople in which you share the needs you have encountered and your ideas on how they could be met. You can invite the laity to join you in going to meetings where these needs are being discussed. You do this because what is at stake is approval and ownership of the ministry.

In doing this legwork you will discover possibilities for ministry that need further exploration. It may be needs of *individuals* such as the unemployed, the blind, abused children, or the dying. It may be the needs of a *geographical area* in a rural county or a city neighborhood. In either case you must involve laity as soon as possible in order to encourage ownership. You may recommend the creation of a lay committee to investigate the needs and develop a report. If possible, a layperson should serve as chairperson. Your role will be to support the committee.

When the committee is ready to report, it is too soon to ask for a decision. Patience at this point will bear fruit. There are some things that can prepare the people. The report can be sent out in advance. You should assume that only half of those at the meeting will have read the material, but this will ensure that the report is not a total surprise. It would be wise to suggest in advance that there will be no vote on recommendations. You should be prepared to benefit from the questions asked and suggestions made. These questions will help identify where the recommendations are not clear or well thought out. Some suggestions will strengthen the proposed ministry. This entire process is part of the way to invite the congregation to own the ministry.

When you are ready to present a plan for a vote, two extremes should be avoided. One is to present a completely detailed plan with the only option being to vote it all up or down. This does not invite ownership but asks people to buy into what others own. The other extreme would be to make vague, general statements, for example, to ask endorsement to help the migrant workers who stay in the community in the winter just because the church should care about them. The church body considering such a request will seldom experience ownership, because there is nothing to own. These extremes are so blatantly weak that you would never use them. However, it would be wise to check to see if your proposal at points resembles one extreme or the other.

As a rule, you should not present the proposed ministry to official decision-making bodies. Instead, laity from the committee should present the report and recommendations. A church, for example, that had asked a committee to see what could be done about a community housing problem has appointed people with knowledge and skills related to housing to study the issue and bring in a report. Once the committee's recommendations are ready the laity should become the advocates for the proposed ministry since the goal is lay ownership.

When a service ministry is approved, this action should be communicated to the congregation to invite their ownership. Printed announcements, minute speakers, and a commissioning service are some of the ways to invite the congregation to be a part of this ministry through their prayers, gifts, and their service. Once the ministry is under way, periodic reports by laity in the Sunday bulletin or church newsletter will nurture congregational ownership. *People can only own what they know.*

A broad-based endorsement by the church's membership will be important for this ministry. Since all of the various constituencies of the local church are needed in some way, you will need to encourage ownership of the ministry even from those who will not be personally involved in it.

The Pastor's Responsibility for the Whole Ministry

The pastoral office gives you special responsibility for oversight of the whole ministry of the church. Even when you are committed to maximize the role of the laity, responsibility for the whole ministry will be yours.

Your unique position in the local church will give you a broader perspective. You know more people, more about all the programs, and will know more about the lay service ministry than any other individual.

You perform a representative function on behalf of the congregation to those outside it. You have authority to speak for the whole congregation, which no layperson has. At times this function can be delegated to others, but the role cannot be transferred. The laity understand this. The role is a given and you must learn to live with it. The role confers upon you the responsibility for the total ministry of the church.

Information will confer influence and obligation. You are at the center of the congregational communications network. You do not know everything, but a great deal of the communication in a local church travels to, from, and through you. Because of this, an important task in helping laity help others is to keep all the sections in touch with one another. This will reduce misunderstandings, even if they cannot be eliminated completely.

Do not expect to be able to speak with authority on every specific detail of a ministry. If you could, it would be a sign that you are doing too much or the laity is doing too little. To interpret the place of the ministry in the life of the congregation is your responsibility. *You do not have to seek this responsibility, it will find you.* In sermons, talks, announcements, or informal conversations with individuals, you will be sharing the purpose and nature of the ministry of helping others.

The responsibility of interpreting the ministry and informing people about it never ends. The time will come when you will find it difficult to believe that you have not told everyone about the ministry! Then to your astonishment you will discover someone who has not heard or does not know much about the ministry. Combine this with the fact that ministry is dynamic and changing and it becomes clear why your role of interpreter is never finished.

The major administrative coordinating task of a lay service ministry will also be yours. You will be continuously identifying laity who can serve in this ministry. Many will seek you out to explore participation in the lay ministry as a way they should exercise their faith. Because of your knowledge of the laity and the ministry, you will be able to suggest ways for people to use their gifts in helping others.

Every church needs a "traffic cop." You are in a position to reduce unnecessary conflicts in the lay service ministry and also to interface it with other programs in the congregation. Any reduction of unnecessary conflict will help keep people's efforts and attention focused on the major concerns of helping others. In this capacity you can render an important service.

Many of the organizations in the congregation will want to know how they can serve in the ministry. You will be able to give suggestions because of your knowledge of what each organization is able to do in terms of their resources and interests, and this will contribute to the effectiveness of the lay service ministry. Sometimes you will be responding to requests. There will also be times you will be able to take the initiative by making a request or suggestion. When you do this, you are not taking the ministry away from the laity. Rather, it is a way that can facilitate lay involvement. Since most of this work is behind the scenes, *the more effective you are, the less you will be noticed.*

When you decide to help laity help others, the first thing you realize is that this decision requires you to prepare yourself before you can help the laity. There are, of course, costs and benefits. Your primary cost will be time—in this case, time to prepare to guide the laity into a lay service ministry. No promise can be made that deciding to help laity help others will mean you will always have less to do. It may mean that what you do is different. On the benefit side there is the possibility that more will be done for others and laity will have a significant and meaningful way to exercise their faith commitment. When that happens, you will feel good about your ministry.

4

What Is Possible
Where You Are?

If you doubt the significance of your work as a pastor, you can be helped by John Naisbitt's book *Megatrends*. He says that fads start from the top, have a short life and little lasting effect. Trends, however, usually start from the grass roots and are more likely to shape the future. Working with your people on human needs in the community can shape the future.

What Are the Unique Needs Where You Are?

Fervent exhortations for laity to help others will yield little but frustration. This frustration can be reduced if you first listen to people in the community.

Since people like to talk about what they know, you can always start by listening to them. The way to begin is to ask questions, such as:

What needs do you see in your community?

Who is working to meet these needs?

What could our congregation do to help?

Could you recommend three people to whom I should talk?

This process will be informal in the beginning. Tentative conclusions will emerge, but you need to guard against prematurely becoming an advocate of a particular ministry. You can screen a range of issues and then allow the laity to concentrate their investigation on a few needs the church can meet.

With some initial ideas you should begin by talking in depth to people about a particular need. They may be laity in your church or people they know. It will not be too difficult to find people who have a good reputation for meeting the need in which you might be interested.

It will be important to ask everyone with whom you talk, "If I could read only four books, subscribe to one magazine, investigate two studies, and visit two places, which ones would you recommend?" You cannot expect to become an expert, but you do want to take advantage of the wisdom experts have to share.

There may be pastors whose laity are already working on the same needs you have identified. They will take time to talk with you. This will help because they understand what motivates and constrains the church. Their suggestions will be beneficial.

You will be amazed at how many resources will be discovered in a few weeks. The problem will be to sort out all the information.

One thing you should do is question the obvious solutions. If something seems so clear and no one else sees it, you need to ask, "What have I missed? Have others tried it and discarded it? Are there problems I have not discovered?" If your ideas seem obvious, you must ask, "Why is no one using them?"

A congregation may want to provide summer jobs for inner-city teenagers. It is a real need. People may be willing to hire them. However, transportation may not be available. Insurance policies may provide no protection, and the youth may feel that the jobs pay too little. A very good idea is stillborn.

Because one way to help will not work, it does not mean you cannot find a way that does. You now see problems that have to be overcome, and you have a clearer picture of what needs to be done.

A ministry to improve a neighborhood may want to make home ownership a way to help both people and the community at the same time. However, in many places where it has been tried, most who took advantage of such a program did not see themselves as home owners. It was a way to reduce their monthly rent. They still thought of themselves as renters. It was a good idea on paper, but in practice it did not work. A good housing rental program could be more effective.

There is the possibility that what did not work elsewhere could work where you are. Learning from the mistakes of others may enable you to create a ministry that will work.

After a rigorous process of winnowing, there will still be more ways to serve than you can possibly handle. These needs are significant to those who have them, and the ministry that could emerge to meet them would be important. Still, not enough hard data exist for a final decision on which of the needs to meet, but informed hunches merit further exploration.

How Are Needs Being Met?

Once you decide to explore a particular need, it is important to inquire how this need is now being met. You almost can take for granted that you will be a latecomer.

There will be surprises! One surprise is that so many have helped so much, and you wonder, "How could I have missed all this for so long?" The advantage of this discovery is that there will be many places to turn for help. Community and university librarians can help locate studies on the issue being explored. Your representative in Congress can open doors to help you find the right government agency and the studies it has commissioned.

Failures are worth investigating. You will want to know why a previous effort failed. Was it underfunded? Did it lack staff? Were the staff and volunteers well trained? Did those who sought to help have adequate skills? Did the people who were to be helped know about the service? Was it underutilized, and if so, why? If you can find answers to these questions, you can avoid an approach that is not feasible. Then everyone gains even though nothing is done! Failures in other places may also contain the wisdom you need to help laity help others.

One excellent way to begin is to find out who is doing well in meeting these needs in your community. You want to talk to them. You will learn a great deal, and in a few weeks you will have established a working relationship with others who are concerned about the needs you want to address.

A word of caution. Many of these people have labored with inadequate resources, little appreciation, and much criticism. They may even be wary of clergy and churches because of some experience that disappointed or hurt them. If you talk to someone who feels this way, it would help if you did the following: *Refuse to be defensive. Assume those you talk to care about the people they serve. Take for granted they want to do a good job.* You will be right more often than wrong. Besides, they have information, experience, and knowledge you need. They can help.

The people you talk to will usually not be able to offer too many specific ideas on what you can do. Some are unsure what the church can do. Still it is important to ask. Asking conveys an attitude of respect that will help in the future. Some of their suggestions will at least point to critical needs.

When you approach people about serving the needs of others, some may suspect a "hidden agenda." "Is this pastor out to make a name or a reputation for himself or herself?" "Is this a new way to get members for the church?" "Will these people be reliable, competent, and helpful?" "Am I going to have a group of 'do-gooders' on my hands who will cause more problems than they solve?" It reminds you that you have to earn their trust.

Since people have been hurt before, doubt, cynicism, skepticism, and apathy are not always pathological attitudes. They may have grown out of hurt and disappointment. People want to know, "Can I let myself hope again?" Sensitivity to the fragile nature of the spirit of those you want to help is a mark of theological maturity.

Your conversations will benefit those with whom you talk. They will be pleased that someone cares. As you make the rounds the word will go out: "He cares," or "She listens." You will not be dismissed, but will be welcomed.

Freedom to move among the structures of society can give you a knowledge few possess. A pastor concerned about rising teenage suicides will talk to many people to see the whole picture. She discovers gaps, duplications, and people working at cross purposes. Because of the trust she has established, she may be able to bring all parties together in a creative way to deal with teenage suicide, thus making a significant contribution because of her role.

You have freedom to touch and influence society's structures. By developing the contacts and establishing credibility with those in these structures, you will have made significant progress toward beginning to help laity help others.

What Resources Are Required?

In order to keep your idealism and realism in creative tension, you will need to ask two questions of a ministry for your church: "Will this ministry be significant enough to challenge us to give our best?" "Do we have the resources to be effective?"

Both questions must be answered positively to enable you to help laity help others. What you are searching for is that point where the realities of time, resources, abilities, and commitment indicate that what you promise to others can be delivered.

To ensure a good beginning ask about available resources. A congregation that wants to help the deaf obtain assistance in learning to live independently may realize no one has skills, experience, or training to work with the deaf. This does not mean the proposed ministry will have to be given up. Instead, a trained person has to be found. Is one available? If so, obtaining this person becomes part of the plan. If not, someone may have to be trained in order to train the laity. It is critical at this stage to know precisely what can and must be done. Now you know what you have to do. This is the real value of asking what resources are required.

First efforts to determine what is needed will underestimate the length of time it will take, the hours needed, the number of people required, and the money necessary. There are two explanations for this: a lack of experience and a strong desire to serve. Allowances can be made for this. Before you start, it would be safe to increase the estimates of all the resources necessary by at least 50 percent. Then the projections will be more realistic.

What you do in the beginning may seem insignificant. You begin to ask yourself, "Is this worthwhile? Wouldn't these resources do more good if used for something else?" These questions are always important, but you need to remember this is the beginning of a ministry. Even the champion runner had to learn to walk. It was a small but necessary beginning.

It is sobering to remember that ministry to others is an intentional intervention in people's lives. It will make a difference. You hope that as much good as possible will be done and as little harm. Most of all, you want to make certain that any promises made have a reasonable chance of being kept. *The future of the ministry hinges more on small promises kept than grand promises made.* Starting a lay ministry to others this way helps to assure that the ministry will live within its means.

One of the reasons for starting a new ministry on a small scale is the recognition of the inevitability of mistakes and misunderstandings. When the ministry starts small, these setbacks can be managed. Expecting difficulties will help prevent your becoming too discouraged when problems arise and will provide you with the courage to tackle them.

Ministry by people, for people, and with people calls for patience and persistence. The demand for both will be enormous, supply will be limited. Ministries can survive and grow in spite of and sometimes because of these stresses. Knowing this in advance can help you cope under pressure.

What Resources Are Available?

How can you find the lay resources available? In a small church you will know most of this information. When a church has more than two hundred members you cannot rely on memory alone. You need a systematic way of ascertaining and utilizing available resources.

The best resource is your members. You will need to know about them. A "talent bank," which is an information record of the talents of the laity, should be created. It will help you to know where your members work, what their occupations, training, education, and hobbies are, which organizations they belong to, what special interests they have, and the ways in which they would like to serve the church. This information enables you to know the lay talent available when specific needs arise.

When you create a talent bank, you will need to create a means of access to the information collected. In small churches an alphabetical card file system can work. For larger churches, card files can be developed for each occupation, hobby, or interest, etc. If a computer is available, this information can be input for easy access.

The big job is to collect the information! A small lay committee can be recruited to manage the talent bank. When they have completed an information collection form, ten laypeople can fill out the proposed form before the congregation uses it, to be sure it does the job. Good advance publicity describing the purpose of the talent bank, and telling how the information will be used is crucial. The form should be mailed to the membership and also should be available for one month at the Sunday services as well as at church meetings. At these times you can see that the talent bank is explained and can ask for the forms to be filled in. Telephone calls to those who have not responded will increase the number of responses. New members should fill out a form when they join the church. For many reasons you will never have all your members in the talent bank. A 60 percent representation of your membership will provide an adequate and significant number of lay resources.

When you discover information about a layperson that may help the ministry, write a short note to file in the talent bank. This procedure would benefit the entire church program by making the information available to others. It would also reduce the number of times people would need to contact you. Increased effectiveness makes this a worthwhile investment of your time.

If you were investigating the possibility of building high-rise apartments, one conversation with a member who sells elevators could quickly let you know if it would be financially feasible. It might be the only occasion you ask this individual for his or her help. At that time, however, the help would be vital and critical, and the layperson would have had the opportunity to make a valuable contribution.

Inviting laity to help the church help others will always be needed. Asking for help from the pulpit, in the bulletin, and in newsletters will inform but not obtain the required human resources. A talent bank will help you know exactly whom to approach with a specific request to help with a particular need. This, in the long run, will not only save a great deal of time but will enable you to help the laity help others.

It is also necessary to ask what *facilities* are available. What are the *financial capabilities* of the church, taking into consideration outside resources as well as the budget? How much *time* do the laity, the pastor, and the staff have to offer? Do these potential resources indicate that the congregation possesses a sufficient base on which to build a service ministry? This appraisal will not in itself reveal whether a ministry can begin, but it will aid in the determination of what ministry is possible now.

Resources are available. Usually there are more than you initially imagined. A distinctive ministry stimulates people to try something new. Some may want to change the focus of their volunteer work, while others who did not or could not do other jobs in the church may now be willing to assist.

People will respond. They will see this as a way to serve Christ, their church, and others. Your basic challenge will be to match the people to the ministry and plan a ministry that will have the people needed to make it work.

When a Ministry Is Chosen

It is seldom possible or desirable for you to select a "prepackaged" lay service ministry. Each ministry responds uniquely to a particular need at a certain time with a definite set of resources. Therefore, helping laity help others will need a custom-designed ministry.

There will still be several options to choose from after you have explored the needs of the community and discovered the resources available. The necessity of saying no to some needs that deserve to be met will be the cause of some difficulties as you and your laity try to decide what to do. No congregation can do everything. To try would be to fail at everything and succeed at nothing. Knowing this does not eliminate the feeling of uneasiness in saying no to some needs in order to say yes to just one. The final decision will disappoint some in the church and many in the community. You have to accept their feelings and your limitations. Until you do this, it is impossible to choose a way to help laity help others in a significant and effective manner.

When the choice is finally made, it helps to remember that even if you had all the resources needed to do everything you wanted, the ministry would still have to start on a small scale. A rural area could need many kinds of medical services. If a prenatal clinic were the most urgent need and an attainable goal, it would be wise to begin with this rather than attempt to meet every medical service need at once. To do the latter would only lead to frustration, while the former could provide a basic service and possibly lay the groundwork for a future expansion of medical help.

Because everything will be new, accomplishing things will

require more effort. For instance, making contact with a person to set up a meeting to discuss problems of illegal immigrants may take days or weeks when the ministry begins. After you have established relationships and a track record, one phone call could arrange the same meeting. This is an inescapable fact of life. You must live through it. It will be easier for you if you do not overextend yourself in the beginning.

Limited accomplishments could create a morale problem when a ministry to help others begins. The laity may depend upon you to provide a great deal of encouragement. The primary reason for this is the laity's deep commitment to help people. This strong desire to help usually generates high expectations. If you have and can help your laity to have realistic expectations, you can reduce the possibility of a morale problem. You will have to support the laity in being realistic. The survival and growth of the ministry depends on it. Dreams, hopes, and goals for the long-term need not be abandoned. The prudent approach is to help the laity set short-term objectives that can become stepping stones toward the long-term goals. A church may have decided the community needs a "big brother" program and seeks to get one started. It begins by working with only five boys, but gains needed experience and helps these boys. This modest start could lead to the creation of a community organization that could be serving hundreds of boys in five years.

Finally, integrity is critical to any ministry that helps laity help others. Integrity encompasses more than just honesty, good intentions, and pure motives. It is a commitment to fulfill promises with as high a degree of excellence as possible. That is why you will take the time to research the needs in the community and see if the needed resources are available or can be attracted to help. No matter how urgent the need, you and your people must assess whether you are able to do what will be required. *Integrity in serving others means to promise what can be delivered and to deliver what is promised.* Only a commitment to this kind of integrity will enable a ministry both to serve and to witness. Realism is the exercise of a responsible faith.

Challenge, excitement, stimulation, and satisfaction are experienced when you decide to begin a new ministry to serve others. It will be shaped by the perceived needs and the gifts, imagination, and commitment you and your laity bring to meeting the needs of others. The challenge for you is to provide the leadership that will bring the needs and gifts together: this is an art.

5

Designing
a Lay Ministry

Two requirements are needed for a lay service ministry to get under way: dreams and details. Without a dream of a ministry to others nothing will be attempted. Without attention to the details the dream will never become a reality.

Usually pastors stress dreams and laity ask about details. These are two sides of the same coin. The challenge you face is to bring these two requirements together.

That you should not have the primary responsibility of carrying out the details is not to denigrate their importance. It is accepting your limitations. You do have a responsibility, however, to see that the "nuts and bolts" issues are addressed.

Creating Clear Objectives

In order to develop a lay ministry to help others, you must have a statement of purpose. It should not be long or go into operational details. Its function is to give direction. Some examples might be:

> Establish a grief support group for parents who have lost a child by death.

> Provide alternatives to the bars for the college students who work in our vacation resort town in the summer.

Select one area in a third world nation and assist in meeting the hunger needs there.

The statement of purpose should be only one sentence long, with no dependent clauses. It states the dream. Then it is possible to work on details and create clear objectives.

A good objective will have several distinguishing features. It indicates *who* will accomplish *what result* by *when* at a stated *cost* of time and money.

"Create a committee to help laid-off workers find jobs," would be a weak objective in a ministry to help the unemployed. While it indicates that a committee will do the work, it does not state how many will be helped, when they will be helped, or what resources will be required. It is challenging, but helping people find jobs may be beyond the committee's abilities.

A clear realistic objective could be, "The employment sub-committee will create a six-session job counseling program in which 50 percent of ten unemployed participants will develop a job search strategy by June 30 at a cost of 100 person hours and $200." The responsibility is clear. There is a *ministry result,* 50 percent will develop a skill. The costs are included. The outcome is within the control of those doing the ministry. A good objective helps those who help others to be clear about what they plan to achieve.

There may be resistance to writing objectives. People may be reluctant to do something new. Some will feel it hinders the Spirit. Others will think caring and compassion are difficult to measure. However, *some important results of a ministry are measurable!* They should be identified.

Some believe measuring a ministry's results misses what is important because we may only measure what we can easily count. You can avoid this by creating *challenging objectives.* Since a lay ministry is prone to try too much, and not too little, this will not prove to be a serious issue for you.

Some may resist because writing an objective may seem to be an unnecessary frustration when they want to start helping people. Nevertheless, your quiet insistence on having clear objectives is one way to be sure that what is done will help.

Laity are busy and will want to know what is expected of them. Young mothers, for example, may be able to volunteer to serve in a church's ministry to meet the needs of other young mothers. They will want to know what they are expected to do and accomplish. Clear objectives meet their needs.

Objectives help you know if you are *doing the right things and not just doing things right.* Let's return to the objective of helping the unemployed. At the end of the program it could be asked if the unemployed took part. If not, why not? Were 50 percent able to develop a job search strategy? Did the program stay within its budget? If not, was the budget unrealistic? These questions can be answered only if there are clear objectives. These objectives will help you determine whether you should discontinue or continue a ministry and where to strengthen it.

New ministries seldom work perfectly in the beginning and older ministries cannot remain the same indefinitely. The role of clear objectives is to help a ministry become and remain effective; to give it a sense of direction and a capacity to make corrections. Seen in this light a commitment to help laity help others indicates that creating clear objectives is mandatory.

Accountability and Authority

Balancing accountability and authority is a very difficult task. Creating an organizational chart is one place to begin. Doing this helps you see if the parts of a ministry relate to one another. It enables you to detect where responsibilities overlap and where no one has a responsibility. Since cooperation is essential, an organizational chart will help make clear who has the authority and accountability for the various aspects of the ministry.

You may feel that you are tinkering with organizational machinery instead of helping people. Experience indicates that to neglect this only postpones decisions that will have to be made until laypeople are locked in conflict over authority or responsibility. Since you will eventually have to resolve these issues, it is better and easier for you to do this in the beginning.

Every ministry will have communication problems. The problem is often not people or personalities, but the nature of communication and organization. *Effective communication in an organization is a real accomplishment.* That is why an organizational chart is so important. It will help you to answer the question, "Who needs to know?"

It would be better for us not to assume that communication has taken place because people talk with one another. To ensure that communication has taken place means you must concentrate on listening. This can be modeled when you respond to others by saying, "Let me see if I have understood what you have said." Then you can share your understanding of what was said. Or when you share your ideas with laity you can inquire: "I want to be sure that I have been clear. What is your understanding of what I have been sharing?" This may seem awkward at times. However, you should neither underestimate how difficult it is to communicate nor how much more difficult it is to correct a misunderstanding at a later time.

Often, what is interpreted as a personality conflict is a structural problem. When there is conflict it would be a good idea for you to ask, "How are we organized?" There may be a problem with the structure that causes a lack of clarity about who is responsible. If this is the source of the problem, then the valuable contributions of able people can be retained by changing the organization. If the structure is sound, then the issues of personality and performance can be addressed.

Another purpose of an organizational structure is to facilitate problem solving, because it will be clear who has to be involved when a decision is made. It also makes a contribution by reducing the probability of overstaffing or understaffing. When a ministry is understaffed, people will send signals that they need help. The problem of overstaffing is more difficult to detect but is just as serious. When there are too many people, they will feel they are not needed and are wasting their time, and will soon leave.

This would be a waste of human resources that could help others.

When new persons join the ministry, they will be able to assume their roles with a minimum of disruption when responsibilities and authority are spelled out for each position. No organizational design can completely eliminate crises. However, a good design can keep them to a minimum. It will enable you to turn to the right person for help. If someone calls to say there will not be enough money to meet next month's bills, you will know whether this is the responsibility of the finance committee, a church board, or the church treasurer. Having a well thought out organization will save you time and effort. Routine matters can be easily assigned to the appropriate person. You will then have the time you need to concentrate on the unique issues.

You will also find it helpful to ask, "What kind of organization will this ministry need if it grows?" Is there a way to structure it so that it will facilitate growth? One way you can explore this possibility is to ask "What if?" questions: What if more come than we expect? What if they need more help than we planned? What if they wanted us to do more than we are able to do? These "What if?" questions are seldom raised, much less answered. They should be. The answers will contain the clues for what you will have to do for the ministry to be able to grow.

You will have an important role in seeing that these organizational issues are worked out. Laypeople will, of course, be involved. Their insights will enhance the structure that is created. Since they will have to implement it, you need their participation. However, you will always evaluate the organization by whether it helps laity help others. If, when, and where it does not achieve this goal, you will change the organization.

Start Small but Plan to Grow

When you begin to help laity help others, you may experience a conflict between your head and your heart. Your heart feels real needs, while your head recognizes limited resources. *The crux of the issue is to be sure that promises to help can be kept.* Small promises that can be fulfilled become the building blocks for doing more in the future. Ministries can grow and mature. Therefore, starting small is only a question of how you begin.

When a ministry starts, everything is new. This presents a large learning agenda for everyone. There is little experience. What one day will be a simple routine will take a great deal of thought, energy, and time. You and the laity will be mastering the basics. Once this is done, you will be able to handle the problems of growth.

Ministries have stages of life. Theodore Lowi has observed the stages that historical movements go through—which is instructive. The four stages he describes in *The Politics of Disorder* (Basic Books, 1971) are "spark of life," "status to contract," "the group," and "Jesus, don't come back"—or the charismatic stage, systematization, standardization, and the bureaucratic stage (pp. 32–61). Each stage needs leadership in order to go to the next stage.

The *charismatic stage* depends on the vision and energy of a few people. You will be one of these people. Charisma is neither a style nor personality, but the tireless labor on behalf of a vision. You must be everywhere and in everything connected with the ministry. This explains why, even with strong lay support, you will have to make a major commitment of time to start a ministry that helps laity help others.

The move to the *systematization* of the ministry will come early. More people will have to be drawn into the ministry, and your direct role will have to be reduced. Your primary responsibility in this stage is to create structures and organization. On one hand, you welcome this. On the other hand, it will be somewhat difficult. You will no longer be at the center of everything. The excitement will be missed. If you do not take this step, growth will be stymied. Not all laity will want you to take this step. They will be uneasy about losing the security your presence provides. Making this transition will test your leadership.

As growth continues, leadership must be shared with more people. At this stage of *standardization,* your leadership role will become indirect. Some people who join at this stage may not know who you are and what you did to get the ministry going. Rationally you will feel good about this, but emotionally there will be a sense of loss. You must step back so the ministry can move forward.

Reaching the *bureaucratic stage* can mean that the original dream is realized; the ministry can run without you. Knowing when to let go so this will happen is always highly personal. It should be based primarily on what the ministry needs. You will have to make this decision. Laypeople will not feel comfortable in saying to you, "It's time for you to step aside." It is an act of maturity for you to indicate: "I will not always be here. The time has come to design the ministry so I am not needed." You know this must be done. The ministry's future requires it.

While helping laity help others never follows a neat pattern, this schema does help. It makes clear that the demand for flexible leadership falls squarely on the pastor. Your ability and willingness to adapt to what is needed at each step will hold the key to the project's maturation. What you do is critical because the goal of the ministry is not just to start small but to grow in effectiveness and size in order to help others.

What Can Go Wrong—Anything and Everything

One precept that has gained wide acceptance is Murphy's Law, "Whatever can go wrong will go wrong." Ministry is not exempt from this precept. Things will go wrong.

When you assume things will go wrong, the planning steps of George L. Morrisey will prove beneficial. He suggests three questions to ask about your plans (*Management by Objectives and Results,* pp. 107, 111; Addison-Wesley Publishing Co., 1970).

What is likely to go wrong?

How and when will you know?

What will you do?

Your ministry will be stronger if you ask these questions before you finalize your plans. The old saying still holds true, "An ounce of prevention is worth a pound of cure."

Anticipating problems enables you to avoid them. For example, one problem all service ministries experience is that people will not be at meetings. You will need to notify people more than once about a meeting. People forget. Dates do not get on calendars. Mail gets mislaid. A timely reminder three days before the meeting could save the meeting, limit frustration, and keep the ministry moving on schedule.

Even with the best plans there will be surprises. Some surprises will come from laity involved in the ministry. There will be misunderstandings and failure to keep promises. Those you want to help will not always do what they need to do to get help. These surprises will probably upset and disappoint you the most. They may cause you to question yourself and the ministry. These feelings are understandable. In a way you will have to share ownership of your reactions when they are based on your assumption that these things will not go wrong.

Another surprise that may catch you off guard is that of succeeding beyond your expectations. This probably seems like the best problem to have. If twenty-five persons had been expected and fifty showed up, it would seem that your ministry was on the way to success. If, however, you were ready to help only twenty-five, it can be a problem. You would be wise to ask, "What will we do if the response is greater than anticipated?"

It is better to have a plan and not use it than to have no plan and need one.

Lowi's schema can help you to anticipate the problems of each stage. In the *charismatic stage,* there will be a problem with *time.* Because you must be involved in so many things, you may have to decide what you can terminate, defer, or delegate in order to have the time to get the ministry going.

In the *systematization stage,* problems will come from the *absence of clearly spelled out procedures.* Too many people not knowing what to do will create confusion. You will want to take the time to work these out in advance, as it avoids larger problems later on.

The *standardization stage* will present problems as you try to share leadership. Here the *absence of clear job descriptions* with authority and responsibility spelled out will be the chief culprit. Without them some laity will err by doing too much and others by doing too little. Establishing clear guidelines for laity before they assume new responsibilities reduces problems.

When the *bureaucratic stage* arrives, you might think that all problems will have been worked out. Not so! The difficulty at this stage is that you will often be *the last to know about a problem.* You will need to create a so-called early warning system to bring things to your attention in time. This is a fine line to walk of not interfering while still being informed early enough to make your contribution to solve a problem. You will want to create some *performance standards* so when things do not go as planned you will be notified. A case in point could be when the income for the ministry drops 10 percent below the budget target. This can be an agreed-upon point for the treasurer to contact you.

When things go wrong, it is not always unfortunate. You will see where planning is incomplete. It becomes a signal to you that corrections are needed to strengthen the ministry. Needs you have missed may come to light, and then they can be handled.

You can correct most things that go wrong. There is no need to panic. You knew something would go wrong. When you know, you can resolve it and proceed.

How Are We Doing?

Most people would agree that it helps to know how the ministry is doing. In order to do this, you will need to plan how to evaluate the ministry after it is under way.

You will have difficulty answering "How are we doing?" or "How did we do?" if criteria to evaluate the ministry have not been agreed upon in advance. Likewise, without these criteria it is difficult to decide what changes you must make to reach your goals while the ministry is under way.

Asking what is important and how it will be measured will help you clarify in advance what the ministry is to achieve. If a ministry, for instance, is seeking to help the unemployed, what matters most may not be how many people obtain jobs but how many still have a job after three months. Measuring placements without checking retention could mean the ministry is failing when the placement statistics make it appear successful.

What is important about indicators that evaluate a ministry? You will need to decide on a critical few that are central to the ministry. The word "few" should be stressed. They should be easy to track and should not require an unreasonable amount of time to monitor. For instance, in one ministry to preschool children it was discovered that a teacher quality indicator was absenteeism. When attendance dropped, it could either signal the normal problems of illness or that parents and children were communicating unhappiness with the classroom experience. The regular attendance record was an indicator that prompted leaders to examine the quality of the teaching in a class.

For evaluation to be an aid in carrying out an effective ministry as well as in improving it, *timeliness of the information is essential.* In some ministries it may be important to have evaluations weekly. In most cases, monthly, quarterly, or annual information will be adequate. How often to evaluate is determined by the needs of the ministry.

Because there are many ways to measure effectiveness, you will have to depend on more than just one measurement. *Objectives* are helpful, because they enable you to ask not only, "Did we meet them?" but also, "Will we be able to meet them?" The objective can strengthen your ministry by letting you know where you are and whether you need to take corrective action. You can select one of several indicators, such as how many people are being served, whether deadlines are being met, or whether we are staying within the budget.

From time to time your *informal conversations* with laity involved in the ministry will provide excellent information. Sometimes you may feel it is necessary to have more carefully designed *surveys* given to people serving in the ministry in order to have good data to evaluate and in order to help you know how the ministry is doing and what could be done to strengthen it.

Those who use your ministry should not be overlooked. Sound *interviewing* procedures need to be used. Otherwise, you will only hear what you want to hear and those being served may only say what they think you want to hear. They do not want to lose services by offending those providing them. This word of caution indicates that once in a while it might be helpful to use *outside trained evaluators* to gather data and interpret it. They will not always report accurately, nor will they always be correct in all they say. Nevertheless, helpful information can be gathered this way. Since the goal of evaluation is to strengthen the ministry, outside observers may identify a need that you have not seen or for some reasons are unable to see.

Evaluation will help you to complete the "feedback loop" that began with the development of a purpose for the ministry, and then moved to setting objectives, developing procedures and policies, training laity, and serving people. Evaluation is the next step in this process of serving people. It is not outside the process. It helps you answer the question, "How are we doing?" which enables you to begin the cycle once more by suggesting what ought to be planned and done next.

Designing a ministry to serve others is not always a glamorous assignment. In fact, this work usually goes unnoticed when it is effective. You will wonder at times if the energy these endless details require is worthwhile. It sometimes appears to be very far from providing services, but when you remember that your task is not to do the ministry but to help laity help others, then the importance of this work will be clear. If you do it well, laity will be effective in their Christian service to others. Those they seek to help will live fuller and more meaningful lives. If your attention to the details of your dreams has these results, then working on them will be worthwhile.

6

Recruiting
and Training Laity

Because it is a pastoral responsibility to identify, enlist, and
train laity for ministry to others, that does not mean you will
do everything. However, it does mean you accept the responsibility to see that everything is done. This has two pastoral
benefits. The laity are recruited to minister to the needs of
others, and preparing them to do this is also an act of ministry.

The Pastor's Key Role as Recruiter

Before you can recruit laity, you need to know why each
position is needed; you must determine its purpose and the
qualifications a person must have to do the work. Then you can
seek the individual who will fit the job rather than design the
job to fit the individual. It may be necessary for you to make
some adjustments later when the position is being filled, which
should not be done in the beginning of this process.

Knowing what is needed, you can review membership lists
and the talent bank. You can ask others if they know of persons
who have the abilities to meet this need. Bulletin and newsletter
announcements should be used. Someone may volunteer or suggest a person after reading an announcement. There are many
ways to identify people who can serve, and all should be used.

When the list of prospects is prepared it often turns out that
the best candidate is already doing other jobs in the church. You
may have to say: "This is the best person and the contribution

he or she could make is so important that we should ask him or her to serve. If this means we must find a replacement for this person in his or her present position, it should be done." Likewise, you should let the layperson being considered be the one who says yes or no. If you decide not to ask the person, you deny him or her this option.

Sometimes there may be more than one person you could ask. How should a choice be made among them? An examination of their church attendance records and, if you are comfortable with doing it, looking at their giving records will help make your priorities clear. Those with a strong attendance record should be the prime prospects. In terms of finances the question is not the size of the gift but whether they make a pledge to the church and keep it. This information gives an indication of the level of commitment. Those with higher commitment indicators will be more likely to accept the job. Of course, there are exceptions, but remembering they are exceptions underscores the value of this process.

Someone has to ask the person who is identified as a volunteer prospect to consider a position. If the position is a major responsibility in the ministry, it may mean you are the one to pose the question. When you ask a layperson to volunteer, a signal is being sent that this position is important. Sometimes a layperson has a long-standing relationship with the volunteer prospect or a crucial role in the ministry. In these cases laity may be the best ones to approach the person.

Regardless of who does this, the one asking must know the specific duties of the position before inviting someone to consider it. You would rather delay the visit than have someone make a call who does not know what the job entails.

Some, including you, may at times shy away from asking others to serve because the answer may be no. The law of averages indicates that more will decline than accept. People may refuse for valid reasons. Should that happen, the call can still be productive. You can acquaint the person with the ministry, convey a positive regard for him or her, and explore a way for the person to be of service in other ways or at another time.

There are perennial concerns of volunteers which can be anticipated. They will want to know why the ministry is significant. This provides them with a strong faith rationale for the ministry and indicates the importance of the needs you are seeking to meet. They will inquire about the training they will receive. "How much time will it take to do the work?" is a question everyone asks. To suggest the work will not take much time or to underestimate the time required diminishes the importance of the position and misleads the volunteer. Giving a straightforward answer is the best thing for you to do. Laity will also be concerned about the ongoing support they will receive. Again, if you cannot answer these questions, you will need to do more work before you make the call.

When you recruit laity to help others, you are inviting them to continue Christ's work. It is a call to ministry!

Covenant and Contract

When a person is approached to join in the project, it is important to highlight both the covenant dimension and the contractual details of the invitation.

In terms of *covenant* it is authentic to suggest to laity being recruited that they are being asked to consider a faith commitment. You are not trying simply to fill a slot. You are asking them to look at a specific task and to consider another matter: "Is this a way *you* can serve Christ? Is this where Christ is inviting you to serve?" This is not used as a gimmick to obtain a positive response. It is a way to explore the covenantal dimension of the invitation to ministry. What it does is transform the request into a faith exploration. This is a service to those invited regardless of whether they can say yes or must say no.

There are few shortcuts. One-to-one contacts will be required and an appointment long enough to share the need and respond to the concerns and questions of the one being asked to serve. You must prepare for the call. It is important to be able to state with clarity what the assignment is, how it fits into the church's ministry, and what the potential benefits of the ministry may be to those served, to the church, and to the volunteer.

Those being called upon may need time to consider the request. They may need more information. They may want to negotiate the job. Regardless of the assignment, it is wise to agree upon a date to decide. Then you need to follow up by that date for the decision. To pressure a person is not advisable, but to ask for a clear yes or no will be best for all.

The volunteer has a right to know some of the *contractual* details of the commitment he or she is being asked to make. Since the time it will take is often underestimated, it is wise not to give a low figure to obtain a volunteer. If several people say no because the assignment will take too much time, the job may be too large. Then you will have to consider the possibility of creating two positions out of one.

Ideally you will have a one-page job description that spells out the position's responsibilities, authority, place in the organization, and desired results. This indicates that the role is well conceived. The description can be left with the prospective volunteer if he or she needs time to think about it or accepts the position. You should write a follow-up letter to express appreciation for the time spent together, and put in writing your understanding of what was agreed upon. This reduces misunderstandings, and creates a more reliable record than your memory.

There needs to be a definite term of service or, at least, a time agreed upon to examine and renegotiate the assignment. Those being recruited need to be sure the commitment they make is not "til death do us part."

Periodic reviews should be a part of the covenant. Reviews can serve several purposes. In the beginning they assure the volunteers of support and help when they begin. Reviews will be more frequent in the early months of a layperson's tenure, in the early stages of a new ministry, or when a new phase of the ministry is begun. They will be less frequent after the ministry is older and the persons serving in a position are more experienced. The temptation will be to assume that at some point reviews are no longer necessary. This is not the case. A regular review every few months offers the opportunity to ask how the ministry can be enhanced. It also ensures that those who do volunteer are not taken for granted or abandoned.

What emerges from these basic considerations is that you need to do your homework, seek the best candidates, and give them an opportunity to respond after a clear case for the position has been given. The burden is on those who recruit. Since you are the prime person in the process and the ministry to others is so crucial, the value of doing this cannot be underestimated.

Personal Growth Through Lay Training

Spiritual growth is one of the benefits for laity who participate in a service ministry. Training will, of course, cover information about a ministry and the skills needed to serve in it. However, your concern will also be to see that training contributes to the spiritual growth of the lay volunteer.

Since training is for ministry, laity will ask, "What makes this work different from what others do or how they do it?" If your ministry is helping mid-career males work through mid-life issues, how will our program differ from that of a psychological support group? Is it only that you pray and read the Bible? Is it motivation, caring, competency, witness, willingness to risk, or tenacity to stay with a person? It is my conviction that *the difference the church makes is its awareness of the dimension of the spirit in human life.* It is open to the questions of belief, not just what one must have, do, or be, but what one's having, doing, and being means.

You must always remember that this will be a major issue for the laity. Therefore, all training programs will need biblical and theological input; time for laity to share faith perspectives on what they will be doing to help others; opportunities to pray, to reflect, and to meditate; and times to make faith commitments.

The design of training sessions will need to provide ways for laity to deal with these concerns.

There are always insecurities when a person begins something new. Some volunteers will be anxious because they are not sure they will be able to help others. There will be fear that people can be hurt if mistakes are made. Volunteers need to be able to express these feelings. Those who have some experience in a particular type of ministry, like a marriage crisis intervention counseling service, can share their early misgivings and how they were able to cope with them. Other laity may have very positive feelings or experiences. To have these expressed will help build a positive spirit among those preparing for the ministry.

You can incorporate a time in each training session when people share their feelings. Fifteen minutes will suffice in most training sessions. You could ask: "What are you feeling good about in the ministry today?" "What do you feel uncertain about right now?" "Are you experiencing any doubts or fears which you can share?" This sharing time begins to build supportive relationships among the laity.

In a few cases there will be some signals in the sharing time that someone should not be in the ministry. This is not an indication that the training is failing. It is better for people to discover that they are not suited for this particular ministry during the training period. However, the primary purpose of these sharing times is to help those in training to handle their feelings in a constructive way.

The basic purpose of training will be to meet the needs of the laity who will carry out the ministry. There will always be a *body of knowledge* to be learned or reviewed. It will be necessary to provide background information on the need, on the people being served, and on the best understandings available in religious and secular thought and experience on how to meet this need.

There will be information about *procedures* laity will have to know. You can ask, "What will a layperson need to know to do this assignment?" The answers to this question will provide the content of the training program. There also should be a time in each session for people to ask questions. Volunteers will feel more confident and comfortable if they are able to obtain specific answers to their questions.

When lay volunteers begin a training program, *they will want structure.* They will expect details to provide a clear picture of responsibilities and how to meet them. They would interpret the absence of such details as signaling a lack of direction and leadership.

Since there is a readiness to learn when laity begin their training, most will not protest over the amount of information they receive as long as it answers their questions. They will want, as well as need, clearly stated *guidelines* on what to do, why it should be done, and to whom they can turn if they do not know what to do. The most important guidelines will need to be put in writing for learning, review, and reference.

A strong training program will help equip people with the *skills* they need to work in the ministry. It is to that training need that we now turn.

Skill Development: Practice and Role-Playing

Effective lay ministry to others includes both theory and practice. Laity will not only ask you, "What am I to do?" and, "Why am I to do it?" but also, "How should I do it?" and, "How am I doing?" In this section you will explore the lay concern of how they are to do their ministry, and in the next section, how they are doing.

After a training program shares the theology for the ministry, provides an analysis of the need to be met, and discusses the organization and procedures of the ministry, it must address the "how to" needs of the laity. Tasks must be described, the do's and don'ts must be clearly stated. Discussions help make sure people understand. At some point they must begin to try doing. It is like learning to ride a bicycle. An instructor can explain how to do it and demonstrate how to ride it, but at some point the learner has to get on the bicycle and go, or never learn how to ride.

A good training design will include field experiences and simulations of situations the laity will face in the ministry. Laity should not be expected to move from discussions to solo assignments with nothing in between. These "in betweens" of training are extremely important.

Observation is an excellent way to learn. It is possible to have a role-playing demonstration in which experienced persons enact a few simulated events which give those being trained the benefit of several situations that experienced people have encountered. The persons who are beginning the ministry can see how situations, needs, and people are handled. They can ask questions and talk about why things were done a certain way.

In some cases actual encounters may be available in training films or on videotape. These media resources may be rented, purchased, or in some situations made by your group, if the video equipment is available. If this is done, permission to videotape must be given and the rights of people protected. Observation of an actual ministry situation requires sensitivity on everyone's part. It is an intrusion into the private lives of others. Everything should be done to ensure that each person is respected and his or her dignity is preserved.

It is important to have time to discuss what has happened. In controlled training situations it would be wise to have twice as much time to examine what was observed as the time it took to observe it. In the case of a film or a videotape, it would be a good idea to see it, discuss it, and then see it again. When observing an actual situation in ministry such as a visit, an interview, or a meeting, time will have to be arranged to explore the pros and cons of the event as soon as possible.

The persons who are being trained should be given questions in advance which will be explored after the observation. They should be asked to define the issues or problems they observed, state what options were available, give their evaluation of the strengths and weaknesses of the person they observed, and tell what the next steps should be.

A training program is not complete until it includes actual experience in the ministry. *Role-playing* is an excellent way to begin. Those in charge of the training design should write out roles for the laity to play. It is helpful to have a group of three persons participate in a role play. For example, you have designed a service ministry to help academically underachieving students learn about computers. The school principal is skeptical of the church's ability to do this over an extended period or do it well. One person can role-play the principal, another the representative from the church's ministry, and the third can observe. After the role-playing each person can share thoughts about the encounter, what was considered helpful, and what should be changed. It's a good idea for each person to have a turn in the role of the one serving, being served, and observing.

These role-playing sessions will be long remembered. If the church can videotape them, the persons in training will be able to observe themselves. This is an unforgettable learning experience. It would be important for the participants to take time to discuss these videotaped sessions after they see them. There are times when making an audiotape would be best. If the training program is for people who would be on crisis hotline telephones, the audiotape would provide excellent feedback for what is essentially an audio ministry.

A strong training program will move to actual experience before it concludes. *The early stages of ministry and the last stages of training overlap.* Ways will be needed to give laity an opportunity to begin doing the ministry under some form of supervision. It may mean that the volunteer's first assignments will be with an experienced person, but now it is the volunteer who is the actor and his or her actions are observed. It may not always be possible to have someone with the volunteer. Then those who are new need to share what they did in some detail with others, and evaluate the experience. Finally, there will always be a need to have experienced people available to respond to unique situations.

This training process may seem slow and time-consuming, but the time must be taken. To abbreviate the practice training phase of a ministry is counterproductive.

Regular Feedback and Evaluation

Training will be needed as long as the ministry exists. To decide what training should be provided will require you to look at the laity in the ministry. Some will be excellent at providing direct services. They will be good at it and will want to stay at that job in the ministry. Others will be better at organizing and managing volunteers. They should, if willing, consider moving into these responsibilities. You will also see that some laity will need to be moved into new assignments. All will need different kinds of training.

There will always be new problems, situations, and developments that require *in-service training.* It may be to give information on a new procedure in the city's employment program or it may be the need to develop new skills in order to lobby for legislation to clean up chemical dumps threatening the community. Once in a while these changes will come from a time of evaluating the ministry. A concern for feeding the hungry of the world may move from sending money to a relief program to pressing members of Congress to change laws that restrict people in poor countries from earning a living. The new assignment will require new skills. That means training will be needed.

In-service training can help you discover what is taking place in the ministry. You will obtain feedback on the ministry that keeps you in touch. The continuing training sessions will also help permit you to rekindle the original spirit of the ministry. These in-service training events help you check whether a person ought to continue in the ministry.

You need to find ways to help people feel they are part of a ministry which is larger than their individual efforts. You should *hold regular meetings to bring all people serving in a ministry together.* These times together serve to affirm those in the ministry. They can be designed around training needs and issues that the laity request or that you believe are needed. "You are not forgotten" is the primary message of these gatherings.

In-service training is one way to review the basics, restate the fundamentals, look at places where the ministry is not functional, review the routine procedures which people are always forgetting, and seek suggestions on how to improve the ministry. It is also a time to share triumphs and defeats, and to remember your commitments to be involved in this ministry. These are spiritual way stations. They may provide a time for rededication.

In some cases you may do this in one-to-one conversations. At other times there will be informal small groups and discussions. Bringing in an outside resource person will be another way to bring people together for this. All of these methods can be used and should be used. These *training opportunities are a necessity, not a luxury.*

One question on the minds of the laity is, "How am I doing?" Sometimes it is asked another way, "How is the ministry doing?" These questions recognize that a person's growth requires evaluation feedback. This will not happen automatically. Times will have to be set, you will have to prepare and then make sure the meeting takes place. It will not be necessary for you to do this with everyone. Some laity can do this for one another. You need to remember that this feedback is important to them.

When you meet with the laity you can ask them where they think they have been effective and where they would like to improve. You can give your observations from the perspective of the whole ministry. *Holding these conversations is what counts.* It helps the laity, and provides information to you from the perspective of those serving in the ministry. It provides clues that can make the ministry more effective and efficient.

Reviewing the ministry annually and at special times is important. It can combine statistical data and informal conversations with providers and users of the ministry. You need to agree with the laity on what will be evaluated, how it will be done, and who will do it. The role of evaluation is to improve ministry by creating a climate that supports self-examination. What is being sought is to encourage a flow of information and suggestions which will help to improve the ministry. No suggestion should be considered unimportant. All are significant to those who make them. They may prove to be valuable to the ministry, too.

At times someone from outside the church should evaluate the ministry. It could be an experienced layperson or a denominational resource person. There will be compromises between what you desire and what can be afforded. An in-depth review should be considered every three to five years or when the ministry is confronting unique problems or opportunities. Then outside evaluators are especially helpful.

Evaluation usually is neglected because of the urgency of needs that have to be met. Everyone is too busy. You may have to be *the advocate for evaluation* to ensure that the ministry is not only busy but effective.

It is impossible to help laity help others without giving recruitment and training a high priority. It takes time. It will, for example, be difficult to develop effective introductory training programs with less than six to twelve sessions. To plan for ongoing training sessions every three months will take more time. When you calculate the time this will take, only the importance of the goals of helping laity help others justifies this investment. But if you do it, the day will come when you will experience the joy of discovering that more is being done and done well than you could ever do alone.

7

Organizing to Support Lay Ministry

Any activity that needs the cooperation of at least two persons will require some organization. As the number of persons, size of tasks, and range of a ministry grow, so will the need for good organization.

The challenge you face is how to keep the organization as *lean and simple* as possible. Even your best efforts to do this will usually end up with more organization than you would like.

The reason for exploring the question of systems and structure is longevity. An effective ministry will need systems and structures that are not dependent upon any one person.

Creating Routines to Facilitate Ministry

When a ministry of the laity begins, it will be anything but routine. Lack of experience and new tasks confront you and the laity. Expect to go through some turmoil. This need not be a permanent state of affairs, but the job will not order or organize itself automatically.

You must press continually to answer two questions. The first is, "Will we have to do this task again?" If the answer to this question is no, then the task should be completed and nothing more done. If the answer is maybe or yes, it is important to ask before, during, and after completion if it is possible to simplify or streamline it. Once streamlined, it will take less time and there will be fewer mistakes made.

"What is the time cycle of this task?" is the second question. Is it repeated daily, weekly, monthly, or annually? Save copies of material, write out observations and evaluations, and think about how to conserve effort. This way you can create needed routines that are effective and effort efficient.

In the beginning most procedures and job descriptions will be untested. These will need to be revised frequently as experience improves your understanding.

You could encourage this by asking everyone to write his or her own *job description* after six months in a position. Or you can discuss the job with the person, revise the description, and then have it written down. When a person is leaving a position, it would be good to review the job description. A regular procedure to review job descriptions provides a way to ensure that the conception and the reality of the position agree.

When people are new, and someone has to substitute for another person, or you have to step in where no volunteer is available, written *procedures* will help. People resist writing down procedures; the reasons and excuses will be numerous and will have varying degrees of validity. Therefore, you need to identify the few critical procedures for the ministry. Then you must see that they are put in writing and shared. Having procedures in writing will add clarity and will also save time and energy.

After the start of a ministry, the best results will be achieved when you arrange for procedures to be discussed periodically with those responsible for carrying them out. This can encourage laity to seek ways to make their efforts more efficient and stimulate them to find ways to improve the services being offered to others.

Once procedures exist it is important to share them. One approach would be to circulate the new procedures in draft form, asking for comments and suggestions from those who need to know about them and make them work. This may seem like a slow way to create procedures, but it is wiser to do this before finalizing them. They should also be in a book that is easy to obtain.

Routines are necessary because the high energy available in the initial stages of a ministry will not be available indefinitely. You will always be looking for ways to reduce the time and effort required. You are not trying to mass-produce impersonal services to people in need; you are trying to see that more people will be helped and helped more.

One routine that will enhance the ministry is to establish *rituals of celebration and affirmation* of the ministry. Annual meetings, for example, can bring together all those related to the ministry to celebrate the achievements of the past year. The more people that can be involved, the better. They all benefit from visible signs that show they do not labor alone. An annual dinner meeting is an excellent way to achieve this.

Another way to do this is with a *newsletter.* This may be a way in which people with public relations and writing skills can serve the ministry. A newsletter can facilitate communication, give encouragement, provide an identity for the ministry, and help everyone "own" the ministry's accomplishments.

An extremely valuable routine that would bring the leadership of the ministry together is that of an *annual retreat* of two or three days to plan the next three years of the ministry. The opportunity to share in a relaxed informal setting will strengthen relationships, create a sense of being a team, and provide a way to think about the ministry's future. For example, one ministry had grown over several years by developing distinct new programs, all of which were housed in separate facilities. At the annual planning retreat it was decided that the community could be served more effectively if the staff were in one centrally located building. It would promote cooperation and diminish competition. Because the annual planning retreat had focused attention on the future, a building was purchased and staff effectiveness was enhanced.

Opportunities to *celebrate in worship a ministry's achieve-*

ments and service while at the same time providing a way for those in it to recommit themselves to the ministry are essential to its survival. It will enable the laity to become spiritually refreshed and renewed for the ministry of helping others. You should not assume this need will be met without giving attention to it. This, too, must be planned if it is to become a part of the routine of the congregation's life.

Creating Support Systems and Systems That Support

Ministry to others usually starts on a high note. It is a combination of a new commitment, a zeal to help, and a touch of inexperience. It is almost inevitable that people will experience a letdown at some point. It is one of those passages which laypeople in the ministry have to go through. Wisdom dictates that you be on the alert for this period. The only unknown is when it will come.

It is impossible to escape the problems of working with people. Results for those you serve seldom seem to come fast enough or to be good enough. It is almost impossible for the recipients to live up to all of your expectations. Those who receive help are not always gracious or grateful. Imperfect results combined with a lack of appreciation creates frustration and anger in the laity offering their service. Laity may experience a conflict between their former sense of exhilaration and their present feelings of resentment. Of course, this is not experienced universally. It will be the experience of only some.

At first, the laypeople may conceal this from you. It is safe to assume these feelings are present and to communicate that *these experiences and feelings do not invalidate our ministry, but can contribute to our maturation.* These feelings can be touched upon in your comments, prayers, and worship. In informal contacts with the laity it will be possible to ask, "Is anything frustrating you in our lay service ministry?" This question gives permission to the layperson to share his or her frustrations. By listening carefully you will be affirming the layperson and communicating that disappointment does not mean failure. You also may discover that the problem which is frustrating the laity requires your attention and can be corrected.

There are times when it is necessary for laypersons to get things off their chest. If you recognize this, you will not rush to the defense of the ministry, intervening too quickly and possibly short-circuiting this process. Rather, it will be seen as a way to increase the ability of the laity to cope with the times of discouragement while ministering to others. Usually after they have let off steam they will talk themselves back into the ministry.

By bringing laypeople together in groups on any aspect of the ministry, you are putting a *support system* in place so you do not have to be the sole provider of support. The hope is to build a network of support among the laity as well as to strengthen those which already exist. What you are doing is taking advantage of one of the greatest assets available for supporting people in a lay ministry—using the rituals and relationships already in the life of the church: resources of faith that can heal and empower.

You, too, need support systems to help you. Sharing with other clergy engaged in similar ministries can give you perspective on your situation. To know that you are not alone may not solve a problem, but it can make it more tolerable.

In almost every setting you will find laity with experience, wisdom, and spiritual maturity who can help and who will keep your confidence. They are the ones who "weep when we weep" and "rejoice when we rejoice." They are your lay support system, and you should rely on them

You will discover that the task of support is a two-way street. The stories and faith of the laity will inspire and encourage you. When you seek to help laity help others, you will find those in need who by some strange irony do the appropriate deed and say the right word that touches your wounds and heals them. At those times you will discover the supreme gift of support for your ministry to others—the experience of having received more than you have given. Knowing this and experiencing this means that from time to time you will need contact with those served, not because they need you but because you need them.

Integrating Laity Into the Ministry After It Begins

Plans will have to be made to enable laity to enter the ministry to others after it is under way. New participants will start at irregular intervals. New positions will be created because of need or growth.

You will need to encourage thoughtful consideration of ways to train people coming into the ministry. If every training session has been evaluated, you will know what has to be included in a new training program. Using laypeople involved in the ministry as trainers not only will make their experience available to the ministry but will help to build relationships between the generations of laity who serve in the ministry. With that concern in mind, expand your selection of resource people to include those whom it is important for new volunteers to get to know, as well as those who have knowledge and skills to impart.

There is no one way to train volunteers. The method you choose will depend on many factors and vary from case to case. The concerns that you will address are: When will the training be needed? Who will offer it? What will the new lay volunteer need to know? If the person is being trained for a position that only *one person* fills, such as head of a volunteer service to help widows know the benefits they are entitled to under Social Security, you or the person who is to be replaced can do the training at any time. Should there be *several persons* assuming a responsibility at the same time, like the ministry of a cooperative rural parish to establish a network of 4-H Clubs in a rural county, it will be possible to hold formal training sessions for all of them on a regular basis. This does not mean you will do all the training. It does mean you will see that it is done.

There will be a constant need to identify, cultivate, recruit, and develop lay leadership. Since leadership will turn over, you need to be sure that new members joining the church have information about the ministry and are given an opportunity to indicate an interest in being a part of it. They will also need to be asked to provide information for the talent bank so their skills can be tapped when needed. Some people will say they can help in six months or only the next year. You will need to contact these laity again at those times.

As you go about your duties the needs of the ministry will be on your mind; the search habit will become for you a way of thinking about ministry. The thought will always be in your mind, "Is there a way this person's need and the ministry's needs can be brought together to benefit both?"

Every year you should review the laity in the ministry. "Does this person need more training, a change of assignments? Will the gifts of these laypersons be better used in another way? Could they experience personal growth if given greater responsibilities? Do they need some time off, or should they leave the ministry?" Doing this will reduce the number of crises you have to handle because you anticipate them.

Worship presents an opportunity to integrate new people into the ministry through a commissioning service. There may be a regular time in the year when this is appropriate. For example, every fall the ministry of a congregation to third world countries may create an annual task force to research the needs in one country in order to determine what the congregation's Lenten mission project will be. The laypersons who have accepted this year's responsibility can be recognized in the service of worship. In other ministries, where turnover is irregular or small, it may be best to have the commissioning when it is needed.

Handwritten notes from you expressing appreciation to the laity help. These notes can be sent when a person begins or does something special; or they can be sent annually. They need not be lengthy. For example, you could write:

I want you to know how much I appreciate your contribution to our congregation's ministry with the refugee families we are helping. Many thanks.

When a ministry begins, the importance of keeping a record of its *history* may not be evident. Eventually this will have to be done; new people joining the ministry at a later time will need to know the story. It would be wise to ask someone to keep the record of the ministry. This will ensure that the records will be there when the story needs to be told.

Reproducing articles that appear about the congregation's ministry will make excellent handouts. It may be possible to do a radio or television program based on the ministry. If one is taped for later program use, most stations will be willing to make copies available for the church's use at a nominal cost. If there are members of the church who have skills in photography, they can be asked to take pictures of the ministry for use on bulletin boards and in publications, or for the record. All of these media materials can serve to inform and promote the ministry and can affirm the ministry as a way by which some laypeople are fulfilling their commitment to love God and their neighbor.

Laity Who Should Not Be in a Lay Ministry to Others

Of all the problems you will have to cope with in a lay ministry, none seems as difficult as handling the layperson who *should not join* the ministry or the one who is in the ministry but *ought to leave.* When these situations arise, you will become directly involved. This may range from being a consultant to playing a more direct role. Not many people, pastors or lay, feel comfortable handling this, and if the assignment can be passed on or avoided, that will happen. Since you have no one else to whom to pass the problem, it will stop with you.

You must be sensitive to the individual who will have to cope with feelings of failure and rejection. In the case of a lay ministry to others, you cannot only be the counselor to the person involved; you also have to consider the people the ministry is seeking to serve. This consideration is not as evident, but it is nonetheless very real. It is not pleasant to have to make a choice between those serving and those being served. That is why these situations are not easy to face or to handle.

To respond too quickly when this situation arises is not wise. You should not begin by blaming the layperson. The pastoral issue is not to assign fault but to serve the people involved. Ask once again, what are this person's gifts and strengths? Is there a place where he or she can be used effectively in this ministry in order to remain a part of it? The problem may be with interpersonal relations. Perhaps this person works better alone and with math, and could help with the record-keeping or accounting side of the ministry. Is it possible to create a new position that could serve the ministry and use the abilities of the person? If these approaches are not productive, you can consider positions in the other ministries of the congregation. This may provide a way to meet the needs of all. After these options have been explored, it is time to talk to the person who should be guided away from the service ministry.

There is no way to predict how such a discussion will turn out. It is a good idea to begin by asking the layperson how he or she feels about the ministry involved. Sometimes, the layperson may already sense that things are not working out. Perhaps he or she has been afraid of letting down the ministry, the church, or you. When this is the response to your question, you will feel a sense of relief and move on to helping that person work through personal feelings and discover a constructive alternative for Christian service.

Not every situation will work out this well. People may not realize that their gifts are not appropriate. They may think they are productive and refuse to hear what you are saying. Sometimes only after you have patiently heard out their anger will it be possible for you to help them find a constructive solution. The deficiency might be corrected by training, support, or new procedures in the ministry. Certainly these options are worth

exploring. If any are selected, it will be important for you to
have an agreement in advance as to what level of performance
would be acceptable and how all would know it had been attained in order to continue or to begin the ministry. While you
should be open to these options, care must be taken not to move
to them too quickly so that they become an "easy out" to escape
the more difficult alternative.

There will be times when there are no options that will permit
these laity to be in the ministry or continue in it. They may
accept this and gracefully resign, with their relationships with
you and the church still in place. Or they may refuse to resign
and to accept another position that would help them preserve
their self-esteem. When you confront this situation, there is no
choice but to ask them to step aside. This is always a difficult
affair. In spite of all you do to respond with sensitivity to them,
the discussion can end very unsatisfactorily. With firmness you
can indicate that they take a few days to think over the options
and other ways to serve the church. Of course, the possibility
of a graceful resignation is never withdrawn. This will be one
time you feel uncomfortable with all alternatives. Under these
circumstances you should, once more, be careful not to blame
them; it will be a more accurate assessment to say that the
ministry failed to place people in the right position.

If a layperson is not accepted or is removed, there will be
negative repercussions; the ministry and the church could even
suffer some temporary losses. When subjected to unfair criticism, you may not be able to respond because of a sensitivity for
the person who was asked to resign. This is not what you
bargained for when the vision of the laity serving the needs of
others first came—it may be an inescapable consequence of that
commitment.

No System or Structure Lasts Forever

In the midst of change you still try to carry out a ministry
to others as though many things stay the same. This has one

benefit. It encourages the creation of the structures that are needed to provide stability and longevity to a ministry. But from time to time your assumptions will have to be re-examined. This does not invalidate the ministry as much as test whether it can survive to carry out its original purpose to help others.

Therefore, it is always helpful to ask periodically, *"What is different now from when the ministry was started or when it was last changed?"* It is always good to ask this question every two or three years to ascertain whether the needs, the people, the resources, or the circumstances have changed. For example, a ministry at one time served an inner-city neighborhood by recruiting teachers to come and serve in the local schools. A few years after this ministry began, the teacher shortage disappeared and the ministry was no longer needed. However, the houses that were purchased to serve that program were now available to meet the rental housing needs of the neighborhood. The ministry to the community continued because it changed to meet the new situation.

Peter Drucker encourages all institutions and managers to ask a question that would be helpful to you. *"If you were not doing this today, would you start it?"* If the answer is positive, then it is appropriate to continue. If the answer is negative, then Drucker says there is only one option—to stop doing it as quickly as you can with the least disruption. The value of this question is that it helps you to know where to focus your attention on things that need to be changed.

Another way to examine these issues is to ask four questions. The first is, *"What is effective in your ministry and what needs to be affirmed and continued?"* The purpose of the question is very pragmatic; if something is working effectively, you do not want to disrupt it. This question also helps to create a positive climate for the subsequent questions. It will help to give balance to some of the negative answers that will come in response to other questions.

"What is valuable in the ministry and the way you do it, but which, if modified, would enhance the quality of your service?"

is the second question. The third question seeks to identify what is missing in the ministry, *"What would be helpful to do that you are not doing?"* The last question, and it should always be the last, is, *"What is not effective and should be discontinued?"* These questions help the persons in the ministry to have a way to engage in a critical, rather than a destructive, evaluative process of the ministry's systems and structures. These questions will require the use of methods that have been examined in a previous discussion of evaluation (see Chapter 5). Once there are answers to these questions, they will have to become items on the agenda for the ministry.

By having a system of evaluation in place to examine the structures and systems of a ministry to others, a ministry can avoid moving from crisis to crisis. This will help you to run the ministry rather than having the ministry run you. Because of these periodic explorations, it will be possible to intervene in a timely fashion, check the accuracy of your assumptions, and learn quickly so you can integrate what you have learned into the routines of the ministry. All of this affirms the thesis that evaluation is important, even if it is difficult to put or keep it on the agenda of the ministry. It provides you and the laity with the information you need to keep the ministry vital as it serves.

The issue is not whether to have or not to have an organization, but whether your organization enables the ministry to be effective. An organization is at best a good tool. Therefore, when you pay attention to organizational questions, the primary concern remains that of helping laity help others. When it becomes clear that it is not doing that, it has no special sanction that would prevent you from changing it.

8

Paying for
the Ministry

Every ministry will cost something. At some point you will ask the question, "How are we going to pay for this ministry?" The answer given may well determine whether the ministry begins, grows, or continues. This concern will always be with you, demanding frequent attention.

Some ministries will require very little money, while others may require a great deal. Usually the difference is in hidden costs. There is the cost of time, facilities, and equipment even if they are donated. You need to inquire of these donated resources, "Would it be wiser to use this time or resource for another need?" It is always a question of good stewardship of resources.

This chapter, however, is limited to one resource: money.

Why Should People Give?

The most competitive sector of our society is the quest for the charitable dollar. Laity, organizations, denominations, corporations, and foundations all receive endless requests for funds to meet important needs. People ask before they give, "Why should I select one request over another for my gift?" Therefore, you are faced with the reality that even an appeal limited to your own church members faces strong competition. There will be other worthy needs that are being urged on the members of the congregation that merit their support This is what you are up against when you ask for money.

Those who would support your ministry to others will want to know why this ministry is important to people. As a rule they are not impressed with statistics of need or service as much as they are interested in seeing how individuals would be helped by your ministry. They want to know not only that you want to serve people but how your ministry is going to do it. They want to apply their limited resources wisely and where they will do the most good.

The need to state a case for your ministry to others gives you the opportunity to bring needs to people's attention, show them effective ways to help, and demonstrate that their support is crucial. Your best appeals will focus on helping people. You may state, for example, that there are many people without adequate housing and then back it up with the facts, but you will also want to share the story of how one or two families were helped to find adequate housing through your congregation's ministry.

You must take time to write a concise statement that spells out why your ministry is significant; three double-spaced typed pages should be long enough. You should assume the person being approached has little awareness of the need, and you should answer the why, what, how, when, and where questions about the ministry. Facts and specific examples should be used. For instance, two hundred people are looking for work in your community. The story of how the church's ministry enabled a person to find employment should be included as an example of what can be done to meet the needs of many. You should state how much money is needed, when it is needed, and what it will enable the ministry to do for people. Regardless of who writes the first draft, it is important that three to five persons read and review it to ensure that it is clear.

The importance of the statement is apparent when you ask, "How can I share this need with those we want to ask to make a contribution?" Having a short statement on the ministry to others will enable you to prepare specific presentations for potential supporters. When contact is made with potential do-nors by mail or in person, they can be provided with a written statement about the ministry. Whether it is printed, mimeo-graphed, or individually typed is a practical question that has to be answered in each case. This will depend on how much money the ministry has, the amount needed to be raised, and an intuition of how the person being asked will respond. Whatever the decision, the material should always be neat, tasteful, and accurate. It should reflect well on the ministry that is being commended.

Descriptive brochures should be created. They can be mimeographed or printed. There should be a supply of them in the church and they need to be revised every year or two in order to be up to date and have a fresh appearance. They should always contain information about how the ministry can be supported. This would include requests for financial sup-port, how checks are to be made out, and to whom they should be given.

The story of a lay service ministry needs to be told in many ways. You and laypersons can share the story with groups and individuals inside and outside the congregation. Someone may be skilled with cameras and can create photographs or slides with which you can share the story of the ministry. If you have access to cassette or videotapes, these can be very effective; however, they need to be of good technical quality or they could detract from the message. The need to tell the story provides a way that some people can help through their gifts of writing, art, and technical skills. If you can involve laity in telling the story, they will discover the meaning of the ministry, improve the way the story is told, and become the storytellers in many informal contacts in the church and community.

You benefit from sharing the story of how the laity are help-ing others. It helps clarify the unique and exciting contribution of your ministry for serving people, and reinforces your people's commitment to it.

Who Could Consider a Gift?

Raising money to help laity help others requires you to identify where and from whom funds could come. Broad general appeals, which have a place in any fund-raising effort, will not be sufficient.

The best prospects for gifts are individuals. Over 90 percent of giving to charitable causes comes from individuals. The major recipient is the religious sector of our society. Most gifts will come from individuals in the church.

You should not assume that, even when the church budget is difficult to meet, money is not available from members for helping the laity help others. In fact, those most likely to respond will often be the more generous supporters of the church budget; you know who these people are. Some pastors choose, for personal or pastoral reasons, not to know what people give. Even if you take that approach, you will have a feel for who they are.

There are two questions to ask when individuals are being identified as potential donors: "Who is committed to this type of ministry?" and "Who could consider a gift to support it?" You can meet with a few leaders from the congregation and review the church membership from the perspective of these questions; the church members thus identified are primary prospects. They will be receptive to an appeal because it is their church's ministry, they know about it, and can see how their gifts help others. Not all who will be asked will support the ministry, but there will also be a few surprises of unexpected gifts.

The local church budget is always a potential source of funds. As a church program the ministry has a claim on the congregation's resources. You will need to give the program support in the church's budget decision process. When a ministry is included in the annual budget it is validated, and this can provide the financial foundation for the ministry. It is also a way for all members to have a part in the ministry through their regular giving.

You should not assume that local church budget support will be automatic. The congregation should be viewed as a donor, and all the work you would do to raise funds outside the local church you should do for the congregation.

Most churches will not be able to budget all the money needed for a ministry. Here you and your lay committee will have to make a judgment. Is it better to seek budget support or authorization to ask for support from members, or some combination of both? As a rule it would be best to seek budget support and permission to make appeals to individual members.

Some ministries will be able to obtain support from *foundations and corporations*. The key criteria for this support will usually be that the ministry is in the geographical area served by them and that it is a service offered to all people rather than to a sectarian church program. There may be, of course, some foundations that are exceptions.

How can these be identified? In terms of corporations, a visit to the United Way or the Chamber of Commerce is the best way. Larger corporations have a staff that handles corporate gifts; they are usually willing to learn about ministry projects that help others. If they can support the project, they will ask for a proposal. It will not need to be long, but must include a detailed budget of income and expenses. Some corporations will be able to provide the time of staff, equipment no longer needed, or products at a reduced price or as a gift. If help is not available, continue to make periodic contacts. Next year they may be concerned about the needs your ministry is meeting.

Large community foundations will be well known, small ones may not be. The best sources of information are your local librarian, the United Way staff, or the development office of a hospital or nearby church college. They have current research publications that list foundations by state, giving the names of people to contact, the foundation's interests and geographical service area, and a few typical grants awarded. Foundations follow these guidelines. Usually, they want short proposals, limit their support to one to three years, and want to know how the project will be supported when the grant ends.

There are times when *the congregation's denomination* has some special funds for helping ministries. These will be small grants for a limited number of years. They should be used for short-term or one-time needs. Here you can contact denominational staff on the local, state, regional, or national level.

Government agencies are also possible sources of funds. Conversations with elected, appointed, and civil service officials would be the way to begin looking for grants. Other pastors who have developed similar ministries can often guide and direct you to possible funding sources. Government agencies often require extensive documentation and are very slow in response and payment; they are also highly political. The proposal will still have to stand on its own merits.

All of these sources have some advantages and drawbacks. You will have to decide whether it is best to accept the funds under the conditions stipulated. There will be times when you will not seek or accept funds because the terms would restrict the ministry's freedom.

Someone Must Ask for a Gift

There is less hesitation in asking for help from a foundation, corporation, government agency, or denominational program than from an individual. In each of these cases, an individual is not being asked to give his or her own money. However, when it is a question of asking individuals to give, most people do not like to ask other people for money.

Why are people reluctant to ask? Three reasons stand out. First, many people feel they are invading another's privacy. Second, they have had enough experience with "hard sell" approaches associated with fund-raising and that makes them feel uncomfortable. Third, they do not want someone to tell them no, because they will feel rejected or that they have failed, or both. These obstacles affect you and your laity.

Whoever is going to ask for a gift will have to come to terms with these feelings in order to be able to ask for a gift. You may have to work through these concerns personally before you can be supportive of laity who will do this. Experience suggests it can be done.

A gift to support a ministry to others offers people a way to serve Christ and the neighbor in need. The intangible benefits of giving more than offset the financial cost. If they do not, the gift will not be made. Your church's ministry offers an assurance that the people the donor wants to help will be helped. It provides a way for them to act on their faith. When you ask someone to give, you help them help others.

You tell the story of the need, but the donor decides if he or she will support the appeal. How people respond is their own responsibility, not yours. It takes three to five prospects for every gift. Probably more will say no, but every yes makes it worthwhile to ask over and over. You will discover that hearing no does not damage relationships or undermine anyone's self-esteem.

Many small gifts, which should be sought, will come in response to mass mailings, bulletin announcements, and general appeals. The preferred approach is to have the direct appeal made by the laity themselves, with strong support from you.

For larger gifts, the contact must be personal. The approaches, in order of effectiveness, are a personal call, a telephone call, and a personal letter. The latter two should be used only if the personal call cannot possibly be made. You may make the call alone or with a layperson. Sometimes laity will be able to make the call. It needs to be carefully planned. If you are seeking a very large gift, more than one call may be necessary. It may require a call to explain the ministry, a time to arrange for the person to see the ministry, and an effort to find a way for the donor to be involved in the ministry. The cultivation of a large gift requires the same care that is given to those the ministry is seeking to serve. It is a ministry to donors.

Someone must ask for the gift! For you to call and ask may give the layperson a chance to share things in confidence that would not be shared with other laity. *You may be asking for a gift, but it is still a pastoral call.* You may feel that a pastor should not ask for any gifts, because the layperson will feel under pressure. This probably reveals more about you than the layperson's perception of the call. However, I would urge you to make the call. You are not taking from people, but giving them a way to be a part of the church's ministry.

There will be times when a layperson is the best person to ask for the gift. Long-standing relationships, trust, and experience may dictate that the assignment be given to a layperson.

When laity decide to give money to help others, they are putting their faith to work. The gifts that will support and sustain a ministry come from love and care for God and others. To ask for those gifts will bring joy to those who ask, to those who give, and to those who receive.

How Can People Give?

It is not possible to go into detail about each way to make a gift, but you should be aware of these options and then ask accountants, lawyers, bank trust officers, insurance underwriters, and development officers of nonprofit institutions for help in understanding and explaining them.

The most common gift is a *cash gift* or a *cash pledge,* which may be made over a period of time. It is possible to ask for cash gifts through *special appeals,* or periodically to invite people to make a gift of a definite amount for special needs. For instance, one church has a 5-10 program for ministry to others. Many members agree to respond with at least $10 to not more than five appeals for funds every year. Each appeal has a specific need to help others. Over a few years this program has raised several thousand dollars to help others. Another way to make a cash gift is with *credit cards,* VISA or MasterCard. Someone at a local bank could help you see if this is feasible for you. If there is a decision to go ahead, it will take two or three years for people to get accustomed to using this method.

One way to give a gift is to give an *appreciated asset.* This may be in the form of stocks, bonds, or property. This gift should be given directly to the church and the church should sell it. The donor does not pay any capital gains tax and obtains a charitable deduction at the current value of the asset. For example, Mrs. Brown bought one hundred shares of XYZ stock ten years ago at $25 a share. Today she gives it to the church to help others. It now sells for $100 a share. Mrs. Brown makes a gift of $10,000 and gets a tax deduction of $10,000. She pays no tax on the $7,500 the stock has appreciated. A word of caution should be made here. If the asset has lost value, the donor should sell it and then give the cash. This is not as complicated as it sounds. Accountants or stock brokers who regularly do this can and should explain this to you and the donor before a gift is made. The best time to ask for this kind of gift is before the end of the calendar year, when people are considering their year-end tax situation.

Another way to give that has appeal for older persons who want to make a gift yet still need income is a *gift annuity* or a *charitable trust.* Such a gift can be larger than a cash gift. The church, however, may get only 50 percent of the gift if the money is needed immediately. To do this it is necessary to ask an insurance company to write an annuity policy in which the church pays the premium from the gift and then uses the balance for its ministry. Otherwise, the church will have to wait until the death of the donor to receive the funds. Because these gifts are irrevocable, those who give receive income for life and obtain a charitable tax deduction that can be used immediately. The income from an annuity is based on age. With a trust the income is based on a return agreed upon in advance between the donor and the church. It must be at least 5 percent. *Donors need to know that if they should need the money they gave, it would not be available because of IRS regulations.* Many denominations have programs that would enable laity to create annuities or trusts and name the church's ministry to others as the beneficiary.

A ministry to others can also be supported through *wills.* This may be the way a layperson can make his or her largest gift. These gifts can create endowments that will provide funds for the long-term support of a ministry. It is important to give information regularly about placing the church in one's will. A news item in the bulletin or church newsletter when the church receives a bequest is an excellent time to share this possibility, or run a line from time to time in the bulletin: "Remember the ministry of the church in your will." You need to help people word their bequest so that a congregation is not locked into a program that may not be needed in twenty-five or fifty years.

Remember that many people want to help others, but their circumstances vary. They need to know that there are several ways to give. There is a way that is appropriate to each layperson's circumstances.

Because many people want to be responsible stewards of their financial resources at all times in their lives, they will appreciate these options for expressing their faith through their gifts. Since information on these various ways to help others may not be known, you will be supporting the entire ministry of your church when you share this information.

Recognition and Use of Gifts

The most overlooked way to obtain funds for a ministry to help others is by thanking donors for their gifts. Giving may be one of the responsibilities of good stewardship, but this does not mean the donor is required to support your ministry. Either you or a layperson related to the service ministry will want to write a thank-you letter. It may be necessary to set a dollar gift figure to decide whether a standard letter or a more personal thank-you letter should be used. That point may be at $25, $50, or $100. You should see that there is a policy to provide guidance. If the donor wishes the gift to remain anonymous, a handwritten letter of appreciation from you is one way to say thank you and honor the request. A donor who gives and is properly thanked will often continue to support the lay ministry to others.

If donors will permit it, gifts can be publicly acknowledged even if the size of the gift is not mentioned. This may be done when gifts are given as memorials, or done in annual reports where donors are recognized along with others who have served in the ministry, or when a special gift of extraordinary significance is made, or when a will, annuity, or trust is received. Reporting gifts will encourage laity to consider a gift and offer suggestions of various ways they can help others.

It is important that proper records be kept of all gifts, and that standard accounting procedures be used for all financial matters connected with the ministry to others. Accountants and bookkeepers can help you help others by providing a service to the ministry that preserves its integrity and reputation.

You should not handle these funds, sign checks, or have this responsibility handled by fewer than two laypersons. As long as you and the laity involved in the ministry protect the donors, the users, and the recipients of monies, you will have made an important contribution to the financial soundness of the lay ministry.

Every year there should be an independent audit in order to protect those who accept the responsibility of managing these monies. An audit does not question people who handle money, but safeguards their reputations and that of the ministry.

Not all gifts should, can, or will be accepted. You are not required to accept all gifts. At times this may create some problems for you, but they will always be fewer than the ones that will follow if an unwanted gift is accepted.

However, *once the gift is accepted, the conditions and terms of the gift set by the donor must be honored.* Gifts are a trust. You cannot divert them to other purposes. If a gift creates an endowment that restricts its use to the income it earns, the principal cannot be used. What this underscores is the importance for you, where possible, to discuss these issues with a donor before a gift is made to ensure that the donor's intent to help others can be followed now and in the future. This cannot be emphasized enough. A congregation may find itself with resources after a few years that it cannot spend because the need for which the money was given no longer exists but a service ministry to others that is very worthy lacks resources. Funds cannot be transferred to other purposes without the donor's consent, regardless of the merit of the cause. For most gifts, which are immediately used, this is seldom a problem. When gifts are for a longer period, these concerns must be addressed.

All of these financial matters underscore your role in the church's responsibility of paying for a ministry to help laity help others. It is a way you serve those who want to help and those who are helped. The use of resources seeks to respect the needs and integrity of all.

Many laypeople can, want to, and will support financially a significant ministry to others in and beyond the local church budget. Many of these people will serve in other ways as well as by giving money. However, some cannot. They want to be a part of a ministry helping others but find that the only way they can participate is by giving money. *Giving is a way to enable them to be in ministry to help others.* It also provides some of the needed resources so better services can be provided to those being served.

Paying for the ministry to help others is an integral part of the ministry. It plays a very critical role because often you are limited in what you can do for others by the available financial resources. With some imagination, hard work, and a great deal of faith, *finding these resources need not be an insurmountable obstacle.* It will require that you give attention to paying for the ministry so the laity will have the resources they need to carry out their ministry of helping others.

A Word
of Encouragement

I have sought to share a comprehensive picture of what you will have to consider and do to help laity help others. When you look at it all at once, it can seem overwhelming. My hope is that this will not lead you to say, "If this is what it takes, there is no way I can do it." It can be done, and you can do it. It is not necessary to do everything at once. As with other tasks of ministry, you do it a day at a time and go step by step. I believe that knowing the issues before you begin will make it manageable.

As I faced long hours, hard work, and a few frustrating problems, it was good to remind myself that you have to walk before you can run. Many of our first efforts were considered insignificant by others. In time, however, it was these early efforts that made it possible to do things we never dreamed of when we started. Where you begin is not as important as what your beginning makes possible.

I remember a crucial turning point for me in our ministry to help others. I realized one day that I had to decide whether I would just help people or help others to help people. The former would limit what could be done with my own resources, but the latter approach would be limited only by the resources we could tap. I chose the latter. I never had reason to question that choice.

The concern that haunted me the most was, "What will happen when I am gone?" It seemed to me that no matter what we would be able to accomplish while I was present, the test of my leadership would be when I was no longer there. As I write this, it has been over six years since I left, but the ministry is still serving people. I believe this result validates what I have suggested to you.

As the ministry progressed and I moved away from the day-to-day direct contact with people being helped, I missed that. There were times when the necessary administrative details, endless meetings, and tedious negotiations were frustrating. It is never the same to hear about how people are helped as it is to be involved in helping them. At the same time, I experienced a profound joy as I watched those providing the help also grow.

When I started to help laity help others I wondered whether there would be enough laypeople who wanted to express their faith this way. There were! I learned that the church has an enormous wealth of talent and commitment in its laity which most institutions in our society cannot match, much less afford.

Finally, my life was spiritually enriched and strengthened. I discovered that faith is an indispensable resource for being able to help others. I was encouraged and helped by the commitment of the laypeople and many of those we served. They all gave me something I could not have attained by myself.

I suggest this experience to you because I believe it is true to the gospel and to our calling to help laity help others. I cannot say to you that it is easy, but I am able to say that it makes a difference in people's lives. I invite you to consider it where you are. I would encourage you to make a place for this in your ministry. I promise that it will not only help those you decide to serve but it will also benefit you and your laity. I trust you will discover these words in Galatians to be the reality of your ministry as you help laity help others.

> Let us not grow weary in well-doing, for in due season we shall reap, if we do not lose heart. So then, as we have opportunity, let us do good to all. (Gal. 6:9–10)

Index

accountability and authority, 65–67
administration, 34–37, 47–49, 67–69

beginning ministry, 59–61

chart, organizational, 65–66
community research, 51–53
congregational ownership, 44–47
covenant and contract, 77–79

donors
church budget, 102–103
foundations, 103
government funding, 104
Drucker, Peter, 97

education for helping, 32–34, 48–49
effectiveness, 19–21, 48, 69–71, 72–74
evaluation, 72–74, 78–79, 84–86, 96–98

failures, 53–54, 69–71
financial appeals, 99–101

giving
asking for gifts, 104–106
use of gifts, 108–110
ways to give, 106–108
Goodwill Industries, 41

hymns, use of, 29–30

Knowles, Malcolm, 33
Kübler-Ross, Elisabeth, 42

lay ministry, 21–23, 29–30, 31, 36–37, 39–41, 45–46
Lowi, Theodore (The Politics of Disorder), 68

Morrisey, George L. (Management by Objectives and Results), 69–70

Naisbitt, John (Megatrends), 51

objectives, 63–65, 73
organizational renewal, 96–98
organizational routines, 87–90

planning for growth, 67–69, 89
preaching, relevant, 29–32

recruiting laity, 75–79, 92–94
research, 33, 40–42, 44–45
resources, identification of, 55–
 59

servant, pastor as, 24–26
spiritual growth, 18–19, 21, 23,
 26, 79–81, 112
support systems for laity, 90–91

talent bank, 57–58, 75
termination of volunteer, 94–96
theological rationale, 39–40, 43
time, 17, 24, 36, 56, 70–71, 77, 78
training, lay, 43–44, 79–84

University Microfilms International, 41–42

vision of ministry, 23–24

worship, 27–29, 89–90, 93